GO!

How to
get going
and achieve
your goals
and dreams
at any age

MARCIA K. MORGAN

Copyright 2018 Marcia K. Morgan

All rights reserved.

No part of this publication may be reproduced or transmitted in any form or by any means, mechanical or electronic, including photocopying and recording, or by any information storage and retrieval system, without permission in writing from the publisher (except by a reviewer, who may quote brief passages and/or short, brief video clips in a review.)

For permission requests, write to the publisher, addressed "Attention: Permissions Coordinator," at the address below.

the publishing CIRCLE
admin@ThePublishingCircle.com

or

THE PUBLISHING CIRCLE, LLC
Regarding: Marcia Kaye Morgan
19215 SE 34th Street
Suite 106-347
Camas, Washington 98607

The publisher is not responsible for the author's website, other mentioned websites, dead or expired links to any website, redirected links, or content of any website that is not owned by the publisher.

The names of individuals referenced in this book have been changed to protect and honor their privacy.

This book is intended to offer women and girls ideas to explore in order to help them reach their goals. If for any reason you feel distressed or need someone with whom to talk, please seek help from a trained mental health professional. This book is not in any way intended to supplement or replace medical advice.

All content is the author's opinion only.

GO! HOW TO GET GOING AND ACHIEVE YOUR GOALS AND DREAMS AT ANY AGE
SECOND EDITION
ISBN 978-1-947398-10-8

Book design by Michele Uplinger

Praise for Marcia Morgan

"The first step of any worthwhile journey is the decision to actually go. GO! is a book that helps us find the confidence in ourselves and take the action necessary to make our dreams a reality."

Nicole Stott
ARTIST, ASTRONAUT

"Morgan's years of experience working with women and girls ranging from disadvantaged teens to corporate executives make her an excellent guide for any woman who wishes to overcome barriers and realize her dreams."

Sandy Cummings
EMMY® AWARD-WINNING JOURNALIST
FORMER SENIOR PRODUCER, NBC NEWS

"Those who read Marcia Morgan's book will be encouraged to identify and strive for new goals and will have the practical tools they need to attain them."

Dana L. Sullivan
ATTORNEY, NATIONAL BOARD OF DIRECTORS FOR GIRL'S INC.

"You may find that the scariest thing is realizing just how powerful you are, how great your potential"

Roz Savage
FIRST WOMAN TO ROW SOLO
ACROSS THE PACIFIC, ATLANTIC AND INDIAN OCEANS

"GO! is an empowering read for women looking for a step-by-step guide to change in their lives, from mindfulness to visualization and action. This thorough examination of how we are wired and how we can break through societal and personal barriers is backed by in-depth research and references."

Gail McCormick
ENGLISH CHANNEL SWIMMER
CO-FOUNDER, JAMII MOJA, EDUCATION, HEALTHCARE
AND WOMEN'S ADVOCACY FOR MAASAI IN KENYA

"All too often we can get in the way of achieving our dreams without realizing that's what is happening. GO! How to Get Going and Achieve your Goals and Dreams provides information and tools to keep us centered, focused and on track."

Jeannette Pai-Espinosa
PRESIDENT, NATIONAL CRITTENTON FOUNDATION
DIRECTOR, OJJDP NATIONAL GIRLS INITIATIVE

TABLE OF CONTENTS

FOREWORD by Roz Savage . . . vi

PREFACE . . . ix

PART I
Goals & Dreams

Chapter 1: How Dreams Disappear . . . 1

Chapter 2: The Power of Objects . . . 9

Chapter 3: The Magic of Mindfulness in Pursuing your Goals . . . 15
What is Mindfulness?
Mindfulness in Working Towards Your Goals
Is Mindful Planning an Oxymoron?

Chapter 4: Exploring Your Creativity . . . 21
Releasing Your Creative Juices

Chapter 5: Capturing Your Goals and Dreams . . . 25
How to Identify Your Goals
Why Women and Girls Pursue Their Dreams
Handling Setbacks

Chapter 6: Those Pesky Roadblocks Women and Girls Face . . . 33
Identifying Barriers to Your Goals

Chapter 7: Visualization with Goal Objects . . . 69
The Power of Visualization and Goal Objects

PART II
Four Easy Steps to Reaching Your Goals

The Four Steps . . . 75

Step 1. Identifying Your Goals and Dreams . . . 79
The Motivation Behind Your Dreams
Who or What Supports Your Dreams?
Your Environment
Barriers to Dreaming Big
Internal Barriers
External Barriers

Step 2. Finding Your Goal Objects and Container . . . 109
The Power of Objects Together
Objects and Symbolism
The Meaning of the Goal Objects' Container

Step 3. Creating and Staging Your Goal Objects . . . 119
Goal Objects: Simplifying and Prioritizing
Decorate Your Container
Putting Final Objects into Your Display
Where to Locate Your Display of Objects

Step 4. Your Action Plan . . . 127
Sample Action Plan
What to Do at Your GO! Display
Rate Your Progress Towards Your Goals!

APPENDIX

Symbolism of Colors, Shapes, and Objects . . . 146

References . . . 150

Acknowledgements . . . 151

About Marcia Kaye Morgan . . . 152

FOREWORD

by Roz Savage
FIRST WOMAN TO ROW SOLO
ACROSS THE PACIFIC, ATLANTIC AND INDIAN OCEANS

I used to dream of having a big adventure. I loved reading books about people climbing mountains, trekking to poles, or sailing around the world. But it never occurred to me that I could have an adventure of my own. Apart from anything else, I lacked what seemed to be an essential prerequisite—a big, bushy beard.

Yes, there was a distinct shortage of female role models in the world of adventure. So, it didn't even take anybody else to kill my dream. I killed it myself, convinced I simply wasn't made of the right stuff . . . an XY chromosome. I buckled down to do what most well-educated women of my generation did: a professional office-based job.

Yet, there was always a mismatch between my outer life and my inner life. After eleven years of faking it and not making it, I was deeply unhappy, conflicted, and unfulfilled. I began shedding vestiges of my old life. I muddled around, trying on various lifestyles to see if they fit. None did, but I learned a lot about myself along the way. My friends probably thought I was in free fall, but I prefer to see it as being just free—free to find out who I truly was.

So, I dreamed big and committed to rowing across the world's oceans to raise awareness of the top environmental issues facing the world today. For a thirty-something former management consultant who had never been to sea before and stood just five-foot-four, this was a somewhat surprising career move. But I was determined. I wrote myself the biggest of all "to do" lists and set about checking off the tasks one by one. Buy boat. Learn sea survival, first aid, celestial navigation, and meteorology. Run, lift weights, and train for endurance on a rowing machine. Devise nutrition plan and buy provisions. Raise money, spend money.

There were many times, even before I reached the starting line, when I ran into obstacles. However, the vision I held in my mind of my dream kept me going. I was going to use my adventure to help inspire people to live more sustainably, and this felt like important work.

The road bumps I encountered during preparations were nothing compared with the challenges of the Atlantic, my first ocean going solo. The weather that year was the worst since records began. All four of my oars broke. I had tendinitis in my shoulders and saltwater sores on my backside. My camping stove and stereo broke, and twenty-four days before the end, so did my satellite phone, severing all contact with shore.

Time after time, I hit what I thought was my limit of frustration, pain, fatigue, sleep deprivation, boredom, and loneliness. Yet, to quit was unthinkable. Even on the darkest days, I held true to my vision and eventually, one oar stroke at a time, I made it across the ocean. I thought back to that first week when I had tried to talk myself out of this crazy idea. I remembered the vision I had of how it might feel to be an adventurer, making a difference in the world, and inspiring people to action.

My process for finding a life purpose, and making it come true, has been a fumbling affair, making many mistakes, and learning things the hard way. The ideas in this book would have really helped me along the way. If you are looking for a life of meaning, Marcia Morgan will take you by the hand and guide you. Using a powerful blend of the spiritual and the practical, this book will help you capture your dreams.

Even with the loving guidance in this book, there will be challenges ahead. Nothing great is ever easy. Yet identifying and pursuing your dreams is the most important work you will ever do. We owe it, not only to ourselves, but also to the world as a whole, to be the most glorious possible version of ourselves.

The rewards will be many. Visualize your dreams. Have faith, persevere, and stay focused on your goals. It will be worth it, I promise you. You may find that the scariest thing is realizing just how powerful you are, how great your potential. Don't shy away from it. Have the courage to be amazing.

Roz Savage

Roz was the first woman to row solo across three oceans (Atlantic, Pacific, Indian) and holds four Guinness World Records. She was National Geographic Adventurer of the Year, appointed a Member of the Order of the British Empire, marathon runner, an environmental leader, and is the author of two books *"Rowing the Atlantic: Lessons Learned on the Open Ocean"* and *"Stop Drifting, Start Rowing: One Woman's Search for Happiness and Meaning Alone on the Pacific."*

PREFACE

The book—just like the journey itself—is divided into two parts.

PART I provides *foundational information* for identifying your goals and dreams as well as for understanding how to maneuver through the common roadblocks that could derail your pursuit. It covers assessing where you are in your life right now and where you want to be, the importance of mindfulness, and the skills needed to handle setbacks and roadblocks. The first part of the book shows how knowledge is power.

The terms "goals" and "dreams" are used throughout the book in a complementary and somewhat synonymous fashion. Although the dictionary defines the two similarly, a dream focuses on a cherished ambition or aspiration. It has a more contemplative and visual component. Dreams are often abstract ideas such as having a rewarding career. A "goal" is more specific and defined, the end-point of a person's ambition or effort. It is the desired result. With the dream of having a rewarding career, the goal might be becoming a high school teacher. Both dreams and goals are important in order to accomplish what you want out of life. One can have a lifelong dream without ever setting a goal to fulfill the dream. PART II presents a more refined use of these terms, but for our present purpose, the terms will be used somewhat interchangeably.

PART II is the *action*. This section walks you through how to create your own display of Goal Objects. It provides four guided steps with activities and provocative questions, such as fill-in-the-blank exercises, to move you towards your dreams. The four steps are:

STEP 1: Identifying Your Goals and Dreams
STEP 2: Finding Your Goal Objects and Container
STEP 3: Creating and Staging Your Goal Objects
STEP 4: Your Action Plan

Identifying and gathering Goal Objects for a display is a central part of the activities. Importantly, it helps you visualize your goals and desired outcomes. You mentally get an image of the future. It supports the saying that you must see it before you believe it. As you navigate through PART II, you will identify and gain insight into your goals and how to achieve them. You may find that you tap into a place, deep within yourself, that has not seen much light for a long time.

Visualization is a well-researched method of goal attainment and performance improvement. Used by many people in business, sports, and everyday life, visualization improves concentration, motivation, and confidence while reducing fear and anxiety. It should not to be confused with some popular self-help experts who say, think about [fill in the blank] and it will simply manifest itself. Nope. Goal attainment involves *both* visualization and hard work.

I developed the Goal Object concept by incorporating the idea of vision boards (cutting out pictures of things you want to do or accomplish and adhering them to a board), with the practice of home altars (a place where special objects are displayed for ritual, attention, and respect) with an action planning process (often used in business). This approach takes your valued dream from a concept, to a concrete goal, to reality.

During this process, you may experience a full range of emotions. As you unearth a newly found sense of purpose, energy, and joy, you may feel outright giddy. You may also experience surprise, fear, sadness, or resentment, causing a few tears. All these feelings are normal. When you are mindful of your emotions and understand where they are coming from, you can use them to guide you in the best direction. That process of listening to your emotions will get you closer to recognizing your calling, interests, passions and dreams.

You will find that working through the four steps in PART II will release your creativity and a sense of play. You may become happier as you get more in touch with your authentic self. Long-held dreams will surface, and you will begin to see what you want out of life materialize before you. Your dreams are there. They just needed to be awakened and nurtured.

These four simple steps can be illuminating and, ultimately, life changing. It certainly was for Liz.

Liz worked hard in the computer design world, yet rarely got noticed by upper management. She was beginning to feel resentful. Instead of getting mad or becoming a "victim," she began doing some of the exercises in this book. She took time to take charge of her life. She stepped back and became mindful of her present circumstances and how those compared to where she wanted to go. She reflected on her goals and what brought her joy. She assessed her work skills and personality. She knew she had a thirst for freedom and a yearning to be her own boss. After this guided soul-searching, Liz realized she wanted to start a business and began the process of becoming an entrepreneur.

Liz carefully selected a ceramic bird (her Goal Object, symbolizing taking flight and soaring) and put it next to her computer monitor where she could see it every day. She was now motivated and on a clear mission. Each day during her lunch hour, she tackled the action plan she had created through the exercises in the book. She started out by going to the bank and setting up her business account. She drafted a business plan, created a web page, and printed business cards. She searched Craigslist for office space and furniture. She became focused and clear about her goal. Seeing the bird every day and visualizing what it meant served as a constant reminder and inspiration. Within six months, Liz had launched her own business and embraced true happiness.

Imagine the power and pleasure you would have in life if you knew what you really wanted. If your personal and professional goals were clear and, in fact, you visualized your goals every day. You could quickly make decisions, identify opportunities, and reduce unnecessary clutter. You and your dreams would be able to thrive in a healthy environment, surrounded by positive, supportive people. You would ignore those little negative voices in your head that create a dam in your stream of dreams. Just imagine all you could do and accomplish!

These prospects are not only exciting, but they can become a reality. Working through these four steps will inevitably change your life in positive ways. When you value your dreams, you value yourself.

Sometimes these changes are significant, other times they are small. All are empowering.

GO!

PART I

Goals & Dreams

MARCIA K. MORGAN

CHAPTER 1

How Dreams Disappear

PRETTY AND PETITE, Christina was a woman who seemed to have it all. Her home was filled with the laughter of two kids and a husband who seemed to adore her. But her sad eyes told another story. She attended a workshop I held in Bend, Oregon, for women who wanted to work on identifying and capturing their goals, dreams, and aspirations. The workshop targeted busy women who felt unfulfilled or who simply wanted more for themselves.

When Christina shared her story, the contours were startlingly familiar, and the other women listening, including myself, nodded along knowingly.

Several years ago, Christina attended college with the goal of becoming a graphic designer. Instead, she dropped out before graduating in order to marry Scott. Shortly afterwards, she started having children, and amidst the chaos and demands of raising young kids, Christina felt her career dreams slipping away. She realized life was *happening to* her. External factors influenced her decisions and personal goals got lost. She married Scott because he had asked, and she dropped out of school because she thought that's what women did once they became a wife. Christina and Scott never really talked about *when* to have children. They had them because it was the time their friends were having them. Of course, there was no question about her love for her children, but she regretted not waiting a few years to start a family so she could have finished college and started her career. Economically, this choice would have been helpful to the family. Emotionally, it would have allowed her to fulfill her dream of becoming a graphic designer. She felt waiting would have enhanced her self-esteem, making her a happier and healthier mother and role model.

Now, Christina wanted to be more mindful when making life decisions. She also wanted to take more control and have a voice in those decisions. Christina felt restless and unsettled, and she hoped to reconnect with her dreams and a lost part of herself.

So did Ellie, another workshop participant. Basketball-worthy tall with shiny dark hair, she exuded strength when entering a room. Ellie shared with the group how she had wanted to be a doctor since the time she'd spent several weeks in a hospital as a little girl. She loved the medical staff, the science, and the idea of helping others and fixing problems. As a young child, Ellie even wore a white lab coat and stethoscope around the house.

When Ellie was in ninth grade, her mother remarried. Her stepfather was an abusive alcoholic who belittled Ellie with toxic words that diminished her self-esteem. She soon began to struggle in school and started smoking marijuana. Her grades dropped. Ellie's lifelong goal of becoming a doctor faded away. She no longer believed she was worthy of her dreams. All she wanted was to get her GED and move out of the house.

For several in the workshop, Ellie's story was heartbreakingly familiar as well.

Both Christina and Ellie and so many others—perhaps even you too—are experiencing what I've come to believe is an epidemic for women and girls: dream drain. It can happen when one is young, as it did with Ellie.

In her work on gender, psychologist Carol Gilligan describes how girls "hit a wall" or "lose their voices" in early adolescence regarding personal goals and aspirations. They may no longer choose to follow their dreams due to peer pressure, an abusive environment, or an interest in boys. Consequently, girls often need special encouragement during these years to avoid losing sight of who they are and what they want.

Dream drain can also happen later in life, as it did with Christina. The demands of life often sidetrack women from pursing goals that could make their lives feel more rich, exciting, and meaningful.

I feel fortunate to have grown up in a family with parents who encouraged me to follow my dreams. Like most kids, my world consisted of what I observed right in front of me. In the 1960s, that amazing new technology called television drew me in like a siren song. Television programming was branching out from the formulaic variety shows featuring long-legged dancing girls and comics who smoked cigarettes and joked about the size of their secretary's chest (yes, *Mad Men* was based on the real zeitgeist of the time). Women on TV were slowly emerging as strong, main characters in nontraditional roles like police work.

My desire was piqued as I sat on a little straw-filled stool in front of the tiny screen. I wanted that interesting, exciting life of the female secret agent, crime fighter, or independent woman of the world who had brains and faced intrigue, all the while doing good deeds. Coifed in a snappy tan trench coat, she had power and panache. I wanted to experience her adventures. The dark underbelly of society—a world so different from my own—became the focus for my yearning: to understand criminal thinking and make the world a better place.

My mantra of "social justice and fairness for women" developed later in college during the 1970s, a period known as the second wave of feminism, and fit nicely into my crime-solving quest. My two passions came together in law enforcement, my first real job. I was director of a special, all-female sex crimes unit at a time when police departments were not a warm and welcoming place for women to work. We worked tirelessly to write sexual assault laws, change policies and attitudes, and give women a voice.

Although I stumbled on a few roadblocks in my career path, I passionately believed in holding onto my dreams.

Many risk-taking, powerful women of my generation opened up opportunities for girls and women today so they could have an equal opportunity to pursue their dreams. Similarly, we stood on the shoulders of brave, trailblazing women who came before us (this supports my theory about why we wore big shoulder pads in the seventies and eighties: so we could stand on each other's shoulders!). Previous generations of women pursued dreams that helped us realize *our* dreams. And our dreams will help our daughters and other girls realize theirs.

Today, opportunities for women abound because many barriers have been lifted. Yet, there are life circumstances that still stymie women and girls who try to move toward their goals. These life circumstances contribute to dream drain.

For over forty years, combating dream drain and helping women reach their full potential has been my life's work. As a sociologist-criminologist, I've worked nationally and internationally with women and girls to help them stay safe and be heard. Several years ago, I began conducting workshops for women and girls of all ages and from various walks of life, from upper-income housewives to drug addicts in prisons. I observed common patterns in what the women told me of their pain and joy, challenges, and successes: they all wanted something more and were willing to go on a path of self-examination to get there. Their powerful, inspirational stories are knitted throughout this book, with their names changed to respect privacy. You will see that you are not alone in this journey.

Some of the women and girls in my workshops were victims of abuse or assault, had experienced trauma, or had been labeled "high-risk" by schools, the courts, or society. Some of them were serving time in correctional facilities or treatment programs. The common thread was that most had lost themselves along the way, their spirits deflated, and their dreams diminished or abandoned on the path to criminality. They had experienced bad relationships, had lived in families where encouragement and healthy role modeling were nonexistent, had suffered ridicule by others, or had put off finishing high school or going to college because they didn't think they could succeed. Some had chosen a life of crime, while others had not. Ultimately, the girls and women had adjusted their dreams to fit their circumstances rather than adjusting their circumstances to fit their dreams.

I've found that women and girls are most susceptible to dream drain in times of transition, such as during adolescence, marriage, divorce, school graduation, moving, tough financial challenges, illness, retirement, death of a loved one, birth of a child, caring for an elderly parent, losing a job, or feeling stuck. In times like these, you can perceive you are suffocating, free-falling, or drifting. Some women have a midlife crisis or simply experience dissatisfaction with the direction of their lives. You, too, may feel invisible or lost, unfulfilled or frustrated, discouraged or empty. The basics of daily life may have left you frazzled and wanting something to change.

Whether due to unsettling external circumstances or churning internal feelings, transition can be scary. Such moments can also present the perfect time to open up, explore, and dig deeply into what you really want, instead of just digging in and staying put. Transitions provide opportunities to explore new avenues that will help you avoid dream drain. What better time to face yourself in the mirror and ask, "What now? What do I want to do with my life?"

No matter what circumstances brought you to this book, it's time now to have an open heart and mind because you're about to embark on an exciting journey of self-discovery. Using the power of Goal Objects, this quest will allow you to:

- reconnect with your buried or lost dreams.
- identify new goals and dreams.

- experience mindfulness as you shape your daily activities in the direction of your dreams.
- be more conscious and purposeful.
- draw from your inner strengths and personal history to shape your future.

Ultimately, you will be happier and more fulfilled. What could be better than that?

GOAL OBJECTS:

A grouping of special objects selected by a woman or girl to represent her goals. Through mindfulness, visualization, and planning, the display of objects becomes empowering and a compass to keep her on the chosen path towards her goals. Goal Objects are an antidote to dream drain.

MARCIA K. MORGAN

CHAPTER 2

The Power of Objects

GOAL OBJECTS (referred to as "GO!" for short) are a collection of ordinary things you hand-select that symbolize your goals and dreams. Through concentration, planning, and visualization, the objects become a powerful way to clarify what you want and how to make it happen. They become a compass to keep you on the path towards your goals.

Goal Objects are displayed in a grouping that becomes a metaphor for your life. When you carefully select objects that symbolize your goals, and focus on the objects, your goals are more likely to be achieved. Your attitude will change. Your behavior will move in the direction of your dreams so your dreams don't fade away. Your dogged determination will emulate 20/20 vision. This tangible representation of your goals clarifies where you want to be, highlights what you want to do, and helps identify the supports you need to get there. As James Redfield said, "Where your attention goes, your energy flows."

People who think about and visualize their success are more likely to achieve their goals. This is the power of Goal Objects. TD Bank conducted a study in 2016 of five-hundred U.S. business owners and over a thousand individuals. In the study, they found that people who used visualization (e.g., boards or pictures) were twice as confident they would achieve their goals as those who did not. Sixty-seven percent believed visualizing goals improved the odds of achieving them. Among small business owners who visualized their goals, eighty-two percent said they had achieved more than half of their goals. Additionally, millennials (a generation raised on electronics and visual screens) were more likely to use visualization than their older counterparts.

Visualization can make things feel more real, more tangible, and more possible. Through visualization, you become more emotionally attached to your goals.

PART II of this book presents step-by-step activities and instructions on how to identify and collect your Goal Objects. Your GO! area might be on your desk, on a table, or by your bed. The Goal Objects might be held in a box, a basket, or a tiny mint tin.

Over the years, I've had the opportunity to travel to over forty countries where I met interesting and inspiring women who assembled their own displays of meaningful objects. These displays had names such as "dream boxes," "shrines," and "altars." Some women referred to them as three-dimensional vision boards. These displays often focused on one or more of the following subjects:

- birth
- death
- marriage
- divorce
- family and ancestry
- friendships and support
- celebrations
- holidays
- achievements or success

- meditation
- passage into womanhood
- peace
- serenity/calm
- transitions/rites of passage
- happiness and joy
- healing
- abundance and wealth
- good fortune
- religion
- goals

For example, in Vietnam one woman's Goal Object sat on a prominent shelf in her home: sewing needles carefully poked into a multi-colored pincushion and surrounded by fresh, yellow flowers. This assemblage served as her inspiration to start her own tailoring business in the village. A Mexican woman selling fish at an open market displayed her objects in the corner of her table, ripe with a symphony of smells. A small altar, proudly positioned on top of a book, enshrined in faded plastic flowers a photo of her seventeen-year-old daughter. "I work to get her to university," the mother said with the grin of an angel. Her dream was to educate her daughter and give her the opportunities she herself never had.

The objects did not give these women special power. The meaning and attention given to the objects helped the women focus their energy and drive.

I was intrigued by the time and thought that went into the many special, almost sacred spaces. Amazing, everyday women with busy lives took the time to create something for themselves. The process of grouping meaningful objects appeared to be distinctly personal, celebratory, and empowering.

Once we become aware of the process, Goal Objects can be seen all around us. Over the years, I've heard from women and girls about displays they have observed in their own family or surroundings. Here are some of observations that have been shared with me:

> *I remember the mantel above our fireplace had all sorts of memorabilia grouped together—my Dad's bowling trophy, my sister's high-school diploma and tassel, our family reunion picture, dried flowers from a bouquet my mom got for her birthday. I guess it's sort of a family display representing joy and achievements.*

> *I have seen groupings of objects in the Catholic Church. Sometimes there is a statue of the Virgin Mary surrounded by candles.*

> *I've seen them along the road where someone died from a car accident. It might have the deceased person's photo, a cherished trinket, a stuffed animal, a balloon, a cross, or flowers.*

> *I never thought about it this way before, but my grandmother had a small round wooden table in her house that displayed special objects. She had a colorful embroidered cloth on the table from her family in Germany. As kids, we were not allowed to touch the table items. It was "Grandma's special table." On the cloth, was her favorite teacup that she would only use when close friends came by. The table also showcased her wedding photo and a few tumbled seashells she had collected at the beach. She loved the beach. All these objects made her happy.*

These are all examples of objects put together to honor and represent something special. They have meaning and significance to the person who assembled them. Look around your own home. Are there photos clustered in one area, or a special collection displayed? What do those things represent or symbolize to you?

Julie, a single mom in one of my classes, wanted to jump back into the job market after ten years away raising her children. She took on a temporary job as a receptionist while she developed her action plan with Goal Objects.

Julie had always loved real estate and could binge-watch for hours on end the home shows on TV. She took her daughter's small dollhouse (that she had long ago outgrown) and literally transformed it into her "dream home." That is, the doll house itself became the Goal Object representing Julie's desire to be a real estate agent.

Each room in the dream home had an object in it that represented an action needed for Julie to reach her goal. One room had the study guide for her real estate license that she would take out and read at the end of her daily visualization time. Being a busy mom, it took several weeks to get through the book. Another room displayed a toy car because Julie knew at some point she would need a better car for chauffeuring clients. Still another room boasted a collection of business cards from local real estate businesses. Julie had begun networking to find a firm to join. The key elements to fulfill her dream were there, all in one place. She approached the daily visualization process with remarkable enthusiasm. Within two years, Julie hung out her shingle to sell real estate—her original goal.

Think about the power of creating a GO! display specifically representing your goals. A Goal Object could be a photo of you running on a treadmill and looking svelte, motivating you to stick with your exercise program. It could be a toy that reminds you of the importance of spending time with your children and family. Combining a display with objects representing health (e.g., empty vitamin bottle used as a flower vase), and other objects symbolizing wealth (e.g., money in a jar) might model the balance you desire in your life. You could group objects in a home section (e.g., a candle) and others in a roam section (e.g., a luggage tag, maps). If you can visualize your goals with the help of these items, that image helps you envision the realization, and you will be empowered to succeed. The possibilities are endless.

A display of Goal Objects also provides a place for quiet, self-reflective time, creating a space for you to stop running or worrying long enough to take care of what matters to you. The objects allow you to concentrate on the positive: joy, goals, strengths, motivations, aspirations, and inspirations. The quiet time allows you to strategize about overcoming the barriers to reaching your goals. Both allow you to become alive with possibilities. Simple objects remind you that you can make things happen. You can reach your dreams!

CHAPTER 3

The Magic of Mindfulness in Pursuing your Goals

Mindfulness can be an antidote to dream drain. Mindfulness is the art of being conscious, purposeful and engaged as a way to create a more rewarding life. Mindfulness can open the mind to think more clearly, thus allowing a more productive shift into planning mode. Mindfulness keeps you focused and on track—make that the *right* track—for you. Keeping your attention in the present goes hand-in-hand with creating a Goal Object display, in that it allows you to see your world and circumstances more fully, make better decisions, and maintain a purposeful direction when identifying and pursuing your dreams.

Incorporating mindfulness into your life can happen at age eighteen or eighty-one. Whenever it happens, you get a fresh start to reboot and recalculate. That is great news! Dreams don't drain away due to age, but they can disappear if you aren't mindful. When you are conscious about your thoughts and actions you know what is going on with you, so you can seize opportunities and deal with roadblocks more effectively. Remember Christina? Lack of attention to her situation throughout the years played a significant role in dream drain for her. She found that life demands filled her time and her mind. In hindsight, she realized she had stopped being mindful and aware of her feelings. Almost unconsciously, her attention had drifted away from her dream of being a graphic artist until one day she woke up feeling unfulfilled, somewhat resentful, and angry with herself.

WHAT IS MINDFULNESS?

Mindfulness means being conscientious and deliberate instead of reactionary. It is staying awake, aware, and alive, while paying attention. It is being purposeful and present in the here and now, while noticing all things around you. To be mindful is to be conscious of all things physically, emotionally, and spiritually *internal* to you. The journey of mindfulness leads both inward and outward.

Being mindful liberates you from clutter or interference. Your concentration homes in on what is important, necessary, and relevant. The focus remains on the meaningful and positive. Mindfulness makes here and now moments special and connected. Even the mundane feels important. You become a keen observer and listener to yourself and others.

Because you stay focused, mindfulness simplifies your life by reducing demands and unnecessary obligations. You can live more fully, effectively, consciously, prepared, and open. Your reality doesn't change. Instead, your relationship with that reality shifts.

In mindfulness practice, you slow down to take a deep breath and listen. This way of being feels less stressful, rushed, pressured, confused, and chaotic. Being mindful can help you feel less anxious and scattered, opening up awareness of unconscious habits and behaviors that neither serve you well nor move you forward.

Living a mindful life is grounding, calming, eye-opening, and centering. From this state of being emerges the passion and joy to propel you towards your dreams. You become adept at identifying and understanding your thoughts and emotions. In turn, awareness of your inner-most workings can bring insight that leads to solutions and helps illuminate the pathway to your goals.

There are many ways to achieve mindfulness in your life. Daily meditation allows you to clear the mind and observe how your emotions and thoughts flow. Focusing on slow, deep breathing calms a wandering mind.

Some women and girls practice mindfulness throughout their day by closing their eyes for a moment to bring their thoughts to the present, such as before eating, talking to clients, taking a test, or typing at the computer. Whether sitting in solitude or on a bus among strangers, you can notice the thought patterns and messages from your body, such as where stress or tension tends to settle. Listening to your mind and body sets the stage for pursuing your goals. When you take the time to listen, your body and mind will tell you what you need and want.

MINDFULNESS IN WORKING TOWARDS YOUR GOALS

Mindfulness sounds pretty amazing, right? So, how exactly does this practice help you pursue your goals? Here are two ways:

1. **You make better decisions.** Women and girls who are mindful make decisions by listening to their heads and their hearts, using both logic and emotion. Being mindful about both elements helps them make better decisions. The most successful women and girls working towards their goals are those who use logic fueled by their passion. They work from the inside outward.

2. **You discover hidden dreams.** Mindfulness is all about being focused and present. The aim is to keep your thoughts from drifting or wandering aimlessly. However, if your mind or your actions feel unsettled, that, in and of itself, can be useful information. Where are your mind and actions wandering to and why? Are your thoughts and actions gravitating to something that brings you joy? Are they revealing a repressed dream or new goal? Maybe your true

passions and dreams lie in the direction your mind and actions keep heading. Listen. Observe. Use the information gleaned to find the best path forward.

IS MINDFUL PLANNING AN OXYMORON?

How can you be mindful in the present as you capture your goals for the future? How can you be in the here and now and yet plan and strategize for the months and years ahead? Traditionally, mindfulness is often viewed as process oriented, not goal oriented.

These are compelling questions, but the answer is yes, mindfulness and planning can, and should, co-exist, but that doesn't mean they can be done simultaneously. If you have not stopped in the present to honestly and deeply think about yourself and your dreams, then you may move along an ill-fitting path defined by others, with confusing maps and unexpected potholes. You might undertake one long trip without having a lot of fun. Being mindful *now* will help you face the right direction for a successful future. Mindful planning points you towards your true north.

Patricia worked in human resources for a large insurance company. Not terribly happy or challenged after ten years, she felt comfortable with her routine and getting a regular paycheck. In her forties, Patricia attended a mindfulness retreat in California at the urging of a good friend. She found that the week helped her be more thoughtful and purposeful about everything she did. She also learned to recognize what she could and could not control in her life.

At a GO! workshop a few months later, Patricia shared an aha moment after she realized how being mindful could help lead her to her goals. She reflected on how her new mindfulness practice had given her clarity about how much of her time was spent out-of-doors hiking in the woods, skiing, and kayaking on crystal clear lakes. Those were her happy places. Accordingly, she selected several Goal Objects which represented being outside (a pine cone, a tiny toy boat, a doll's backpack) and displayed them in a small round basket. She kept her

GO! display near her bathroom mirror so she could see it every day. She wasn't exactly sure where the Goal Objects would lead her, but she intuitively knew the collection fit her well and she remained open. Soon a position for an HR director at an outdoor company opened up with great benefits and an environmentally-conscious culture. Now mindful, open, and receptive to change, Patricia landed the job.

As you plan for the future, think about how your goal makes you feel in your mind, in your body, and in your spirit, *right now in the present*. Are you excited and joyful? Do you want to stand up and dance when you envision your goal? Do you recoil, get nervous, and feel dread? These are in the moment feelings that will help guide you into the future. Mindfulness goes beyond just trusting your instincts; it involves a whole-body experience.

Equally important, your mindfulness practice allows you to assess where you are now in your life. Hold up a hypothetical mirror and ask yourself honestly: Am I happy? Sad? Content? Is this where I thought I would be in my life right now? Why/why not? How did I get here? Be receptive to your unfiltered answers. Think about the good, the bad, and the ugly. How do these factors impact your future?

There are many benefits to being mindful and present as you connect to the future. Lao-tzu, Chinese philosopher and founder of Taoism, said "the way to do is to be." In other words, to do, to accomplish, to move along the path towards your dreams, is to pause and listen. It is to be awake, alert, and mindful. Take the time to be with your thoughts.

Many of the obstacles causing dream drain are societal, structural, and cultural. Having a heightened awareness may not always prevent them, but if you aren't mindful, your dreams may trickle away without notice until they are gone. When you are mindful, you're able to recognize what is going on in your life and take control.

CREATIVITY:
the process where something new and valuable is formed

CHAPTER 4

Exploring Your Creativity

RELEASING YOUR CREATIVE JUICES

Being creative is a helpful skill to develop in the process of reaching your goals. Imagination and willingness to explore and develop new ideas and paths are fundamental. Creativity helps you forge a route that specifically works for you, your goals, and your situation. This amazing skill makes it possible for you to uniquely solve problems as you tackle obstacles along the way. Being creative when selecting Goal Objects can also open up possibilities you may never have considered.

Some women and girls don't believe they are creative, and they feel intimidated by the thought of creating anything—even creating the very life they desire. Fear not! Everyone can be creative, and creativity can take many shapes and forms.

Here are some simple rules to help release your creativity.

- Creativity has no right or wrong. Explore your dreams without judgment.

- Artistic talent isn't needed to create a GO! display.

- Neither your creation nor your process need be "perfect", in whatever sense that means to you.

- Liberate yourself from the expectations and pressures to perform. Practice a little positive self-talk.

- Find a few buddies to share dreams and goals. Some women and girls who create GO! displays get together once a month to share their ideas and progress and to encourage each other's efforts. The sharing can be done in a special group, or the activities might be incorporated into an existing meeting, such as a book club. Creative energy, support, and accountability can come from others.

Several women from a book club shared with me that their discussions around goals and dreams made for one of the most powerful gatherings they had experienced in all the years they had been meeting. The eight women, ages forty-five to fifty-five, met every other month in someone's home over a potluck dinner and wine. The group had built trust and support over time by following the activities and guidelines from the four-step GO! method to facilitate their discussions.

One woman, recently divorced, realized she wanted to take a spiritual trek on the Camino de Santiago in Spain. She found a small Spanish flag, bought hiking boots and a guide book, and grouped her objects in a special corner of her bedroom. She gazed at the objects every day. She set aside time to visualize and make plans to finance her dream.

Another woman struggled with seeing her last child go off to college. The group helped her talk about her sense of loss and changed identity as well as her strong desire to do something for others. Over a couple of meetings, the empty nester realized she wanted to start a horseback riding program for disabled youth. She found a small plastic horse which she kept by the kitchen sink to remind her of her goal. While she did the dishes, she practiced visualization as she gazed at the horse, which symbolized her dream.

- Forget convention or rules, barriers or boundaries. Heaven knows women get plenty of these every day.

- Try journaling. You may find that regularly writing down your thoughts, experiences, and feelings releases creative juices and prevents you from getting stuck. Excavate your mind and creativity. Write your thoughts and ideas—whether on paper or computer screen. Periodically look at what you've written and allow your words to guide you. The more you write, think, and talk about your goals and dreams, the more the creative ideas will flow. Additionally, research suggests that when you write something down, you are more likely to make it happen.

- Let go of the past and say hello to the future.

- Look for the meaning and joy in this creative process. Make a note of what brings you happiness and gets you going and establish your direction from there.

- Let your mind go big and wild and remain open to all options.

- The creative process can be transformative. You may pick up an object for your collection and it suddenly "speaks to you." That is, it represents what you are trying to feel or communicate. The object inspires you and just seems to work in your grouping. Let that creative process lead you.

- You may also pick up an object and think it speaks to you for a while, but then it doesn't so much. Give yourself permission to release it and say goodbye. The creative process encompasses both bringing things in and letting things go. That dismissed object clarified something for you and helped get you to where you are now.

Being creative and trying new things makes me think about the fast food restaurant where I worked in high school. I learned a lot about myself from that experience: (1) I didn't want to smell like onions the rest of my life; and (2) I knew the job wasn't a good match for me personally, for my interests, or for my skill set. Good to know! It served a purpose for me at the time. Not only that, the job motivated me to get creative and pursue my goals.

The more you are open to exploring, looking at possibilities or objects not normally in your purview, and embracing the exercises in this book, the more you will have a rich, creative experience.

CHAPTER 5

Capturing Your Goals and Dreams

HOW TO IDENTIFY YOUR GOALS

We've all had goals and dreams at some point in our lives. Many of these aspirations have been achieved, while others have gotten lost or waylaid. Figuring out what happened to these lost goals and evaluating the reasons they disappeared represents an important step in preventing future dream drain.

What if you can't think of any specific dreams or life goals? Do you feel flat or numb inside because you don't have clear direction or passion? You may feel like your head and heart are disconnected, and the old spark and zest have disappeared. What if you can't even remember ever having *had* that spark? Since you picked up this book, my hunch is that you have the courage to change that scenario. You may have given up or stopped dreaming for yourself years ago. Maybe you grew up in an alcoholic or dysfunctional family where dreams were extinguished. Or, on the other end of the spectrum, you may see the world as a grab bag with so many opportunities to choose from that you don't know which goal to pursue first or where to start.

If any of this sounds familiar, the activities and questions posed in PART II of this book will help guide you. I would bet that you do have dreams. It may take some exploration and you may feel like you are peeling an onion (complete with a few tears), but your dreams are still there. Now is a great time to find those lost dreams or even create new goals for yourself.

A while back, I presented a workshop to a group of high-risk teenagers. The girls asked thoughtful questions about how to navigate their world while pursuing their dreams. Most thought little beyond their day-to-day existence or further into the future. They saw their environment through a lens clouded by significant barriers (abusive home life, frequent school changes, poverty, unhealthy relationships). The girls described their lives as more like a game of checkers than chess, taking one small step at a time and not thinking strategically about the big picture.

The girls completed the workshop activities with the concentration, seriousness, and precision of surgeons. They talked about the heart-wrenching challenges in their young lives and how they yearned to reach their goals even though they didn't know how. One girl told me, "I don't know how to do life." Their life circumstances may have been different from your own, but despite all that, they shared with everyone on this path the same motivation: to find joy and fulfillment by reaching their goals.

Their group leader, a woman in her early fifties, came up to me at the end of the session with a vapid look on her face. "I don't have any dreams," she quietly told me with a combination of surprise and consternation. "I am numb. I realized as I listened to the girls talk, that I am supervising them, yet I'm not a good role model. I ignore my own interests, talents, and inner voice. My passion has flat-lined. I truly want to change for myself and for them."

Many females are socialized to help *others* be the best they can be. That isn't necessarily a bad thing. In fact, that is a pretty great thing!

However, giving of yourself can work as a hindrance if such generosity comes at your own expense. Do you stop going for your goals and trying to reach your potential when you help others? Dream drain! Goals and dreams are not a zero-sum proposition. There are usually enough goals and dreams to go around. It is not a competition for a finite resource. Pursuing your dreams at the same time as other women (including your daughters) can be healthy and infectious.

Whether you are twelve years old with eyes wide open or sixty-two years old entering retirement, the questions you ask yourself about life goals may not be that different:

- What do I want to be?
- What makes me smile, feel good, feel content?
- What brings me joy and wonderment?
- What am I wired or geared for?
- What are my aptitudes?
- What gets my juices flowing, stirred up, passionate?
- What do I naturally gravitate towards?
- What resonates with me?
- What makes me feel fully alive? Creative?
- What gets me up in the morning and feeling excited?
- What allows me to contribute to society in a meaningful way?
- What can I do to reach my full potential?
- What feeds my soul?
- What keeps me curious and wanting more?
- What makes me feel connected and engaged?
- What makes me tick?
- What do I love doing?
- What would I do if failure wasn't possible?

Answering these questions by yourself, for yourself, is important. You may have people in your life who tell you: "Lawanda, you are a great organizer!" or "Marie, you are an excellent cook," or "Janese, you are a wonderful musician." These statements can provide clues to the puzzle as you try to identify your goals, but don't weigh external voices too heavily. You actually may just be going through the motions of cooking or playing the violin. Are those activities a passion for you or for others? We waste a lot of time and energy not being true to ourselves. As females, we tend to put on a lot of costumes and placating smiles. When we finally stop and look inward, we find more authenticity. The energy expended to wear those costumes can be redirected into something more meaningful to you.

Additionally, goals may not always be obvious. For instance, maybe your life-long goal has been to hike Mount Kilimanjaro. Yet you find the idea of nursing school keeps coming up for you when doing the visualization activities. In truth, these two goals may not be mutually exclusive or even conflicting. Pursuing *both* avenues may be possible, such as working with a medical team in Tanzania. Perhaps you always wanted to be an actress on Broadway. Yet, when doing the exercises in the book, you find yourself thinking about fixing up a home. Maybe the only way you can afford a place to live in New York, while pursuing your acting career, is to find a fixer-upper. If you are mindful during this process, you are more likely to recognize multiple goals that under the surface may be complementary.

If you are still feeling fuzzy about your passion and your goals, that's okay. Take baby steps. Find something close to the goal you think you want to pursue and take it for a spin. Try it out. Kick the tires, as they say. Maybe you'd like to get involved in a community project, a nonprofit cause, a volunteer or internship opportunity, or a political campaign. Sometimes, your passion is right in front of you; at other times, you might have to dig deep. But remember, you can't force passion. As you feel, smell, experience, explore, and follow your curiosity, stay mindful. What are you feeling in your body and thinking in your mind in that moment of exploration? It takes time to look outward and inward. Allow yourself time to wonder and the passion will surface.

Thinking about and identifying your goals and dreams is an incredible place to be in your life. As you visualize your goals using the Goal Objects, your passion will translate into concrete, tangible actions.

WHY WOMEN AND GIRLS PURSUE THEIR DREAMS

There are many reasons why women and girls pursue their goals and dreams, but the simple reason is, why not? They have confidence in themselves, develop the skills necessary to undertake the challenge, and create the opportunities that allow the dreams to come into their lives. All this takes hard work and steadfast determination. Successful achievers start by taking time to think about their dreams and then do something to make them happen. The steps aren't complicated, but they do require a positive mindset, time, and commitment. The process also requires understanding your motivations and preparing for setbacks.

HANDLING SETBACKS

You've just hit an uncomfortable and unsettling roadblock. Your gut tells you to give up and stop trying to reach your goal. A natural response would be to retreat to a negative place. That pint of chunky chocolate ice cream calls your name. You clutch a big spoon as if marching into battle. You snuggle under a womb-like blanket on the sofa, watching mindless TV. Been there. Although mighty tempting, there are healthier, more productive responses to setbacks.

Setbacks can hurt and deflate your energy, but successful goal seekers don't let a problem get the best of them. They take time to reflect on both positive and negative experiences in their lives to better understand how to move on. Oprah Winfrey faced abuse, poverty, and even being fired from her first job. In a 2013 commencement speech to Harvard University, she said, "There is no such thing as failure. It is just life trying to move us in another direction."

I met Tanisha when we both were presenting at a national training a few years ago. The youngest of four girls from Atlanta, her father had died in an accident when she was just three days old. "I grew up strong and independent," she proudly shared with me. "My mother was a saint and my role model, working two or three jobs and refusing to take a handout. I got pregnant at fifteen years old and was told by an uncle that 'you'll end up just like all the other girls—no education and living on welfare the rest of your life.' That was a hot button and a huge motivator for me. I was just headstrong and angry enough to prove him wrong. After being emancipated at seventeen, I worked my way through college and went on to get a master's degree, all while being a single mom. I've never taken a dime from anyone. Today I own two assisted living facilities that I designed and built. I make a good living and am fulfilling my goal of helping others."

Tanisha worked hard and channeled her feisty energy in the direction she wanted to go.

Here are seven techniques to get back on track if you hit a roadblock or setback when pursuing your goals:

1. **Take a brief break.** Do something you find restorative, such as taking a walk in the woods or on the beach, surrounding yourself with supportive friends, getting a massage, unplugging (from cell phone, TV, news), doing yoga or meditation, or similar activities.

2. **Be gentle on yourself.** Everyone experiences defeats. Forgive yourself. You are human. View these roadblocks as simply stepping stones to your goals and then embrace them. You can't change the past, but you can learn from the past so you can redirect the future. Holding grudges or dishing out blame isn't constructive. Learn to let go of the past so you can move forward. Nelson Mandela famously said, "Resentment is like drinking poison and then hoping it will kill your enemies." He mastered the art of forgiveness and went on to powerfully and compassionately lead a nation.

3. **Conduct an analysis.** Analyze what happened and scan where you are right now regarding pursuit of your goals. Identify all the things you learned from the setback. For instance, you now know one way that won't work. That is useful information! You may have learned that working with the staff at XYZ company felt negative and

disrespectful. They were not truthful with you and burned you out. Listen and learn from your intuition. Much rich information lies in these setbacks if you take the time to mindfully analyze the experience and how it made you feel.

4. **Review your original goal(s).** Revisit your original goal(s). Do you still want to pursue that endeavor? Did the goal fail you, or was it the route and the circumstances that failed? Do you need to find different or additional Goal Objects to symbolize your changes?

5. **Reinvent yourself.** If needed, create a new course of action. Let defeat be your fuel! What can you do differently next time to avoid another setback? Keep calm, steadfast, and positive. Take your analysis insights to re-create a new approach or tweak the existing one. Here is your chance to be creative. The trajectory towards your goals will be stronger now.

6. **Visualize success.** Get reenergized and reinvigorated by looking at your Goal Objects. Use the objects to visualize where you want to go and how you want to get there. Take time to daydream like you did as a child, with that same freshness and wonder you had lying on your back in the grass staring up to the sky. Transport yourself from distractions and slow down to be fully present with your Goal Objects. Visualization helps spark creativity and helps you get back on track.

7. **Jump back out there and be open to the world.** If you are open to the world, the world opens to you. This receptivity can illuminate a path and present you with options you may never have envisioned. Anything is possible, but you have to be present. Share your ideas and needs with others, allow yourself to be a little vulnerable, and stay open to where the process takes you.

CHAPTER 6

Those Pesky Roadblocks Women and Girls Face

IDENTIFYING BARRIERS TO YOUR GOALS

Why haven't you pursued your dreams? Although your reasons may be complex, your inertia is likely based on plain old fear or self-imposed barriers. By being aware and mindful, you will begin to understand the etiology of behaviors that don't serve you well. So, grab them by the horns and control them. When you understand your own roadblocks to success, you can address them and move forward.

Let's sort through these fear factors as well as other barriers so you can begin achieving what you want out of life.

Barrier: Time, Energy, and Planning

How often have you said, *I don't have the time or energy to do xyz?* You are not alone. Chaotic, busy lives can derail your dreams. One woman told me, "When you're living moment to moment, just getting by, you don't have space in your life to dream." In fact, this is exactly the time you should be putting your energy towards your dream pursuits. How else can you escape that crazy pace? How else can you divert your path from an unhealthy direction you (and maybe your family along with you) do not want to take? Decide what you want, visualize it, and make time to think about those desires daily. Be steadfast and focused, persistent and tenacious. Remember the old adage, "What you believe in, you have time for."

It is interesting how rarely females set aside time or allow themselves the "luxury" (is it really a luxury or a necessity?) of planning and working towards their goals and dreams. You might feel it is selfish to talk about, let alone, pursue your dreams. After all, seemingly more important things to attend to, such as work, school, or family, always present competing demands on your time.

Yet, if you do not take that time, the famous Lewis Carroll saying may come true: "If you don't know where you are going, any road will get you there." Time will pass. Another day goes by. Life is over. There you are.

I appreciate the sage advice given by flight attendants during the airplane safety instructions. They tell passengers to "put on your own oxygen mask before helping others." Here I am suggesting a similar notion. If you do not take care of yourself, how healthy and helpful will you be to others around you?

Carve out time to ponder and pursue your goals. For example, every Sunday night you might get out your calendar and to-do list. Find places in the coming week for fifteen to thirty minutes (or more) to be creative, read, make calls, do research, or whatever you've listed on your goal action plan (you will develop an action plan in PART II, STEP 4 of this book). Think creatively about how to find snippets of time: on the bus/train/plane, waiting at the DMV or the doctor's office, before your children get up in the morning, after school. Block that time in your calendar and consider it sacred. Protect it like you would any other important commitment. Your time is important but so are you, so cherish your special time. If you don't, other things will fill up your day.

How you prioritize your time and energy says a lot about how serious you are about your goals and dreams. Time management directly affects the realization of your dreams. No matter what past conditioning may tell you, *you* control your time. Prioritizing also entails simplifying. As you take time to simplify and declutter those toxic/unhealthy demands in your life, you will find more time for what you really want to do.

Time management involves a series of choices, one choice at a time. If you tend to postpone making choices and decisions, you may be overthinking your strategy, which can be a symptom of procrastination (more about this later). Additionally, delaying action could be a sign that the dream or goal isn't a good fit for you. When the goal accords well with your life and you truly want it, you will make time for it.

Take responsibility for your choices and your priorities. Have you ever said, "I didn't have time to work on my [goal] today; I had to take the kids to buy a birthday present?" In the previous sentence, the words "had to" should be replaced with "chose to." The birthday present could be an excuse or a time management issue. Could your spouse/partner have taken the kids to shop? How about shopping at another time that is more convenient for you? Why was this activity so last minute and urgent?

Only you can decide how you spend your time. You want an organized house, yet you go out with friends to the movies instead. You want to be debt free so you can buy a home someday, but you keep maxing out your credit card with purchases of frivolous things. You want to take a cooking class in Italy, only you haven't spent time searching the internet or contacting someone to find out how to begin. People keep asking you to do things and you don't know how to say no. These distractions steal time away from pursuing your goals. What does this say about how you value yourself and prioritize your time? The more time you spend on your goals, the more likely they will be achieved.

Your life is a mirror reflecting all the choices you make regarding money, food, work, school, romance, and well-being. If you are not choosing to regularly think about your dreams, they will continue to float freely in the ozone. Dream drain! One way to retrieve the goals from space is to gather symbolic objects that depict these goals, reflect on how these objects represent your goals, and set aside time to take action and make those aspirations come to fruition. At the risk of sounding like a one-liner on a bumper sticker, life really is short. You need to make time for what you believe in and what you want.

Barrier: Fear of Failure

Some women stop pursuing goals because they fear failure or the unknown. Uncharted territory may feel risky and uncomfortable. These feelings may have roots in messages females receive in childhood. Girls are often socialized to take fewer risks than boys. Trying something new can feel like a risk because it requires stretching yourself mentally, emotionally, spiritually, and sometimes physically. Interestingly, often more stress, discomfort, and anxiety occur in *anticipation* of something we fear than in actually experiencing that fear. Sometimes, the more challenging (read: uncomfortable or scary) the experiences, the more rewarding their fulfillment.

So, what if you don't finish writing the great American novel by age thirty? Is that a failure? No. Instead, maybe you took writing classes and joined a writer's critique group. Good for you. You pursued your writing passion! Taking smaller steps is more than many people accomplish, and I bet you were jazzed by the experience. You may have learned how the publishing world works and will be poised for future success with your writing goal. You beefed up your skill set and may have met some great people along the way. These contacts might introduce you to a new hobby, new friends, or a yummy restaurant, or they may even invite you to their villa on a Greek island—who knows! By opening your world, the world opens to you. That is not failure.

Each time you have a temporarily delayed success (a much better term than *failure*), the derailment is only momentary. The interlude provides a great learning opportunity if you take time to be mindful. Mindfulness aids your success by allowing you to pause and think about the experience and its lessons. Women who ultimately reach their goals enjoy many temporarily delayed successes along the way. J. K. Rowling was rejected by twelve publishers before her first Harry Potter book was accepted.

Failure can impart a profound lesson if you pay attention. It can help you discern what you want or don't want in your life. The experience can offer insight into your personal strengths, thinking process, behavior patterns, and areas that need work. Nothing else can clarify things in such an acute and intimate way. "When you survive, you become stronger," a forty-nine-year-old woman shared with me one day. You can become smarter and wiser if you take the time to be mindful and not dismissive.

Women and girls who find personal success set aside their fears to learn, embrace challenges, and recognize that obstacles are just part of reaching one's goals. When they encounter an obstacle, they know they can figure out a creative strategy to get around it, or through it, and continue onward to their goal. They understand that achievement takes effort and necessitates channeling their inner Don (or Donna) Quixote to deny the roadblock victory.

Fear often creates *avoidant goals* in women. These types of goals rely on the premise that the absence of a negative is a positive. For example, some women select a goal for themselves that tries to prevent something bad from happening or to avoid a loss. The desired outcome often involves survival, relief, or safety, such as getting a restraining order from a threatening partner, staying at home, or avoiding embarrassment.

Avoidant goals are designed to maintain the status quo. Such goals may be important for safety reasons, but they should not replace your life goals and dreams. Goals need to propel you forward, such as a goal of going to school, joining a club or special-interest group, learning a new skill, or developing a talent. Goals should energize your life and bring you joy. In contrast, avoidant goals are based on fear and try to keep things on an even keel (e.g., not doing something new or different, avoiding certain people or situations because you don't know what to expect, or not asking someone for what you need or want).

As you work on pursuing your dreams and goals, I encourage you to embrace the unknown and the unfamiliar. You will never grow if you stay within the familiar. Endure the discomfort that comes with stretching yourself. Only then can you blaze new pathways without fear.

> *"I have failed over and over again
> and that is why I succeed."*
> MICHAEL JORDAN

Barrier: Fear of Success

You may fear success and believe the cost is too high. You may dread being exposed as incompetent, a fake, or undeserving of your accomplishments. You may fear that if you are successful, others will snub or ostracize you. (Do you really want to be friends with these types of people?) Since women and girls are relational and often define themselves by connections and relationships to others around them, this fear can be powerful. You may also experience anxiety about being unlovable or abandoned by men who shy away from a successful female. If your partner doesn't want to be with an accomplished woman, what does that say about your partner? It speaks volumes. Do you really want to be with a person who thinks this way—a partner who doesn't support your dreams of being happy and fulfilled?

You may feel selfish for having your own goals and dreams. You may think others will see you as a bad mother, sister, or daughter. Aspiring to reach your dreams doesn't automatically compete with your other roles. You can be a great mother while pursuing your goals. Moreover, as I've said before, a healthy, joyful, fulfilled woman makes a great role model for her children and others. If you have any doubts about that, check out some of the excellent literature available on having a healthy work-life balance. Fortunately, as societal views on gender roles are changing rapidly, fear of success is diminishing for many women and girls.

Barrier: Fear of Being Different

A close cousin to fear of success, the fear of appearing different in some way, can trigger fears of rejection and becoming an outcast. You probably remember having these kinds of feelings in high school. Your behavior back then was likely influenced by peer pressure to seek the holy grail of popularity or to be accepted into the right clique. Mean-spirited gossip and bullying also worked to ensure conformity to a value system and acceptable behavior at the time.

Our social environment, whether in school, work, or the greater community, shapes our worldview. For instance, our capitalistic/entrepreneurial culture values making, accumulating, and often flaunting money. This creates a climate where certain occupations hold higher status than others. The media bombards us with messages nudging us down a prescribed path. Consequently, our culture often substitutes materialism as the only way to have a meaningful life. If you dream of working for the Peace Corp helping orphans in a third world country, teaching in an inner-city school, or setting up a food bank for the homeless, you may, as the saying goes, find your heart is fuller than your bank account. That can feel like a disconnection from the mainstream definition of success. Having an unusual dream that goes against the grain can feel challenging and isolating for some women and girls. At the same time, there is nothing wrong with being an entrepreneur or aspiring to achieve financial independence. Being a CEO of your own company can be rewarding. No matter what goals you pursue, hold on to your dreams! Only you can know what feeds your soul and spirit. Dare to be different. The world needs women with a variety of goals.

Barrier: Fear of Looking Inward

Some women and girls fear looking inward through self-examination and reflection. They may not know how to start, what they might discover, or how introspection might affect their world. Some women read books like this one and practice self-exploration on their own. Others may seek the help of a counselor or friend to facilitate that journey. Still others may fear that looking inward will upset the equilibrium they, or their family, now enjoy. What if they discover something they don't like about themselves, their spouse, or their family? *What if . . .*

If you had a difficult upbringing, the idea of reliving it might understandably cause apprehension. You may have stuffed away or compartmentalized those memories. No one wants to experience pain, sadness, and discomfort. If you feel this way, be gentle with yourself. Take baby steps towards your goals. These formative experiences profoundly shape us. Whether you realize it or not, our family history impacts our choices every day. You add up a series of unhealthy choices and the upshot is you have taken a path you didn't want, but here you are. Now what?

The first step entails looking at the total package of your life and confronting the fear of looking inward. Examining formative experiences allows you to reclaim your power. The past influences the present and the future. If you don't understand your past, you are destined to repeat it (and your children will too). If you mindfully make a midcourse analysis and correction, you open your life to fresh, new beginnings.

You may be thinking about going to a counselor but hold back because of doubts. If you feel this way, ask yourself why you're hesitant. Wouldn't you go to a doctor if you needed care for a physical ailment? Seeing a counselor shouldn't bear greater social stigma than going to the doctor for the flu. In the same way that a good friend listening to you offers support, a neutral, nonjudgmental listener such as a counselor can offer objectivity and guidance. Weigh the upside of learning more about yourself with the downside. If the insights gained might help you accomplish what you want more easily, then a counselor provides a good option.

Besides private counselors, there are low-cost alternatives for counseling through local social service agencies, women's centers, colleges, or religious institutions. You can find a resource that fits your personality and budget (cost should not be a barrier). Remember, you stay in control when you see a counselor, and you always have choices. No one is going to make you do anything you don't want to do. Counselors are there to help you solve problems and reach your goals.

One woman shared with me, "When I looked at my own issues and environment, I began to get happier and freer. The counselor helped me look at things in a big-picture way. I started looking up, not down, and that propelled me forward."

Don't let your past or the present pull you down and limit your life options. You are worthy and capable of capturing some great dreams. Don't let them get away!

Barrier: Perfectionism

Ahh... the dreaded P-word. Sometimes you postpone making a decision or taking an action because you think you aren't ready and the end result won't be *perfect*. How can you know unless you try? Is there really a perfect time for anything? What does perfect mean, anyway? Repeat after me: nothing is perfect. Perfection is unattainable. Calculating risk has its uses, but if you believe the moment or circumstances must be ideal before you act, you will freeze in indecision, unable to accomplish anything.

In her 2016 TED Talk, Reshma Saujani discussed how, instead of teaching females to be brave and take risks, women are taught to be perfect. Girls still grow up more protected than boys. They need to experience failure in order to learn to be strong and to realize that not being perfect can be a good thing. Don't be afraid to make mistakes. That is how you learn.

My husband and I have a rule in our home that no one can even use the P-word. Wanting and striving to do things better is healthy. Expecting perfectionism is not. In fact, perfection doesn't exist. Aspiring to perfectionism can prevent you from living life fully, following your heart, and pursuing your dreams. I strongly urge you to drop the dreaded P-word from your self-talk.

If fear of failure and anxiety about perfectionism surface as you work on identifying your goals and gathering your Goal Objects, take time to explore the roots of these feelings. They often stem from childhood relationships such as having a demanding parent or teacher with unrealistic expectations. Work on recognizing the feelings and understanding where they came from. Does that little nagging voice still pester you? If so, take a deep breath, laugh aloud at how these messages don't serve you well, ignore them (say *stop* in your head when you hear them), shake out your hands as if flinging negative energy off your fingertips, pace around a bit, do whatever it takes to bid perfection expectations farewell and replace them with new, healthy attitudes and self-talk.

Barrier: Self-Sabotage

Self-sabotage consists of subconscious acts that hinder your progress towards your goals. You become your own worst enemy. Some women and girls use self-sabotage unknowingly as a way to avoid the pain, humiliation, embarrassment, or disappointment of failure. Self-sabotaging actions erect walls and become a self-fulfilling prophecy.

You may have recognized this behavior in others or maybe even in yourself. Self-defeating behavior frustrates those around you because the actions are often surprising and difficult to understand. You claim you want to finish the photography class, but you drop out during the last week. You say you want to start a business, so you gather lots of information and forms, but you never fill them out or act on what you said you wanted to do. You say you want to design clothes, yet you play video games for hours. Others can see your potential along with your dreams melting away. When this happens more than once (common for someone who does self-sabotage), witnessing the impact disturbs those who truly want you to succeed. Additionally, your support system slowly deteriorates because of the emotional roller-coaster of continually encouraging you to no avail. You work against yourself. Become aware of your self-sabotaging behaviors and replace them with positive self-talk and actions.

Self-sabotaging can also be a symptom that perhaps your goal isn't a good fit.

Self-sabotage can also take the form of giving yourself an out when you are working towards a goal. You might make statements such as, "I'll try", "I'll do my best", and "We'll see what happens." These statements lack enthusiasm or commitment. Many women and girls use this as an emotional safety net—*if I don't fully try to succeed, I will feel less like a failure if I don't.*

It reminds me of the minister's advice at a wedding a few years ago. Throughout the ceremony, the minister kept telling the couple to "keep the bar low" in their marriage. That one took me by surprise. I *think* he meant that we often get skewed, romanticized views from TV and movies that marriage will confer a continual state of bliss. Nevertheless, several of us in attendance were a tad dismayed by this marital advice. I still believe that achieving lofty personal and professional goals ups your game and your relationships with those around you. It is a form of self-sabotage to use the low bar metaphor as an excuse or standard for not working hard. Of course, all relationships have their ups and downs, but does that mean we shouldn't aim for more ups than downs? My husband and I reference the "keep the bar low" advice whenever one of us does something that warrants a good chuckle.

Barrier: Sabotage by Others

In PART II, you will be looking at the people in your life and evaluating whether they are supporters of your dreams, or dream crushers. It is important to have a web of healthy, supportive people in your environment that provides a sounding board and emotional support for you to talk about your aspirations.

Avoid toxic people who don't have your best interest at heart. Be aware of the words and behaviors of others, in particular, when you share your dreams with them.

Research has shown that "social uncertainty", such as being the recipient of bullying by others or emotional abuse by intimate partners, influences the nervous system and the brain. Toxic words and behaviors can sabotage your goal-seeking efforts by depleting you physically and emotionally.

What do you do if your spouse, partner, or family aren't abusive but they simply don't support your dream? What do you do if it feels like they are sabotaging (perhaps unknowingly) your efforts? I have friends where the husband wanted to sell everything, retire early, live on a sailboat, and embrace his inner Jimmy Buffet. The wife, on the other hand, didn't want to leave family, friends, a nice house, or her job. How do you resolve a dream impasse like this? The key is good communication in which you can safely share your innermost feelings. How else can you reach a mutually satisfying compromise? If one person in a partnership feels like they are giving up everything and receiving nothing in return, resentment builds, and I can guarantee smooth sailing won't be on the horizon.

Another form of sabotaging behavior by others is pressure to follow cultural roles and expectations.

I met Isabella when she was working on her master's degree in counseling. A confident, twenty-nine-year-old Latina, she seemed wise beyond her years. She shared with me that as a female in her culture, she was expected to not continue her education beyond high school, to marry, and have children. Instead, she said she had to buck that script and follow "that fire in my heart."

"I had to run with that fire, not ignore it," she said. "Whatever that drive and passion I had was my motivator. I just knew in my heart that all labels and obstacles were surmountable. Being kind of stubborn helped too. Now people label me successful and I decided that label is a good one that I want to keep."

Barrier: Trauma

You may be wondering why I added trauma as a barrier to reaching your goals. Simply put, many women and girls have experienced trauma, yet may not recognize how it can impact their world and the pursuit of their dreams.

A traumatic experience is an experience that threatens someone's life, safety, or well-being. It can be the result of an event, a series of events, or a set of circumstances that are physically or emotionally harmful. The following is a list of traumatic events. These are examples, not a comprehensive list, since trauma is personal and can only be defined by the woman or girl who experiences it.

- Physical assault
- Sexual abuse or rape
- Emotional or psychological abuse
- Neglect/abandonment
- Domestic violence
- Witnessing abuse/violence
- War/genocide
- Accidents
- Natural or human-made disasters
- Dangerous environment
- Witness or victim of street violence
- Historical trauma or current oppression

Trauma can have lasting adverse effects on your mental, physical, social, emotional, or spiritual well-being. Trauma can impact development and health throughout your life and is associated with risk of delinquency, school failure, drug and alcohol use, and crime.

Each woman or girl reacts to trauma in her own way. However, some typical reactions include:

1. Emotional reactions (hyper-vigilance, overly emotional, post-traumatic stress disorder (PTSD));
2. Psychological and cognitive reactions (difficulty concentrating, slowed thinking, difficulty with decisions, blame);
3. Behavioral or physical reactions (sleep disturbance, substance abuse, frequent illness, especially GI tract problems, pain);
4. Beliefs and values (difficulty trusting anyone, lowered self-worth, difficulty in relationships).

Trauma can overwhelm coping skills, cause a biochemical reaction, and even change brain patterns. When a person experiences trauma, the survival responses of *fight, flight, or freeze* take over. The amygdala (the part of the brain that detects fear and prepares for emergency events) can become overdeveloped. The frontal lobe, which controls planning for the future, judgment, decision making, attention, and inhibition, can become impaired. And when the amygdala has to work so hard, the frontal lobe becomes harder to bring online. But the good news is that healing, recovery, and rewiring of the brain are possible.

The Adverse Childhood Experiences (ACE) Study, originally funded by the Centers for Disease Control and Prevention and Kaiser Permanente (1995–97), showed how childhood trauma is linked to mental, behavioral, and physical outcomes. For instance, trauma can impact the adult onset of chronic disease, mental illness, and victimization. The study measured ten types of childhood adversity occurring before the age of eighteen. These included physical, verbal, and sexual abuse; physical and emotional neglect; a family member with mental illness, incarceration, or abuse of alcohol or other drugs; witnessing a mother being abused; and losing a parent to divorce or separation.

The following questions were asked in the ACE Study. If you answer yes to a question, you receive one point.

1. Did a parent or other adult in the household often or very often, swear at you, insult you, put you down, or humiliate you or did anyone act in a way that made you afraid you might be physically hurt?

2. Did a parent or other adult in your household often or very often, push, grab, slap or throw something at you, or did anyone ever hit you so hard that it left marks, or you were injured?

3. Did an adult or person at least five years older than you ever touch or fondle you or have you touch their body in a

sexual way or attempt or actually have oral, anal, or vaginal intercourse with you?

4. Did you often or very often feel that no one in your family loved you or thought you were important or special or your family didn't look out for each other, feel close to each other or support each other?

5. Did you often or very often feel you didn't have enough to eat, had to wear dirty clothes, or had no one to protect you or your parents were too drunk or high to take care of you or take you to the doctor if you needed it?

6. Were your parents ever separated or divorced?

7. Was your mother or stepmother often or very often, pushed, grabbed, slapped, or had something thrown at her or was she ever kicked, bitten, hit with a fist, or hit with something hard or ever repeatedly hit, even for a few minutes, or threatened with a gun or knife?

8. Did you live with anyone who was a problem drinker or alcoholic or who used street drugs?

9. Was a household member depressed or mentally ill, or did a household member attempt suicide?

10. Did a household member go to prison?

Of the 17,337 mostly white, college-educated people with jobs and health care who participated in the study, sixty-four percent had an ACE score of one or more adversities; twelve percent had a score of four or more.

The researchers found that the higher a person's adversity score, the greater the risk of chronic disease, mental illness, and anti-social/criminal behavior. For example, compared with someone who had a score of zero, a person with a score of four or more is twice as likely to smoke, twelve times more likely to attempt suicide, seven times more likely to become an alcoholic, ten times more likely to have injected street drugs, and twice as likely to have heart disease. People with a score of six or higher have shorter lifespans by about twenty years. The cumulative effect is profound. The study revealed a hidden epidemic: adversity factors contribute to most of the major public health issues in our society.

Additionally, research on resilience has shown that exercise, nutrition, being in a safe relationship, having a trusted adult in your life (for a child), living in a safe place, and mindfulness all contribute to a healthy brain and body. Resilience research also shows positive results in schools and programs that help students with high ACE scores increase their grades, test scores, graduation rates, sense of well-being, and hope for the future.

The majority of girls and women in the justice system have high adversity scores. Estimates are between eighty and ninety percent have experienced some form of trauma. Similarly, mental health clients and those with addiction challenges have experienced complex, prolonged trauma. Interpersonal violence, especially at the hands of a trusted adult, is particularly damaging for children throughout their lives.

If you have experienced trauma, you may wish to explore its impact on your life and how it affects the pursuit of your goals. A professionally trained counselor can help you sort through these issues.

Barrier: Learned Helplessness

Sometimes women and girls fall into a pattern of feeling helpless. They think, as well as express through words and actions, that they have no personal responsibility, accountability, choice, power, or voice to do anything about what is going on in their lives. It's easier to blame someone else—a spouse, ex-spouse, boss, friend, child, the government, or a family member—for their current situation or life circumstances.

Blame may be a way to discharge pain and discomfort, but it gives away your power. Blaming others isn't helpful and keeps you stuck. Playing the victim role says more about you, and how you feel about yourself, than it does about the people being blamed.

You are not a victim, nor are you helpless. The good news is that because blaming others and taking the role of victim are learned behavior patterns, they can be unlearned. Even if you live in an isolated community, experience abuse, never went to college, struggled in rehab, or feel too fat or too thin, *you* have control over your thinking and behaviors. Identify what you can and cannot control, then don't waste energy on what you can't control. Are you *choosing* to allow your ex-husband to influence or control your life? Are you still angry about being fired from a job four years ago? Are you ruminating about what your art teacher told you years ago—that you have no creativity? You, my dear, are in charge of your own decisions and destiny.

Victim thinking can become a pattern you don't even realize you are following (unless you are mindful). It locks you into a mental trap, making it harder to reach your goals. No one *makes* you do anything. Everything in life is a choice (except death, taxes, and a few other exceptions). You have free will. The only way to get unstuck is to start putting your head in that non-victim space. When you do, your self-esteem will improve, and you will feel stronger. I also guarantee your world will open up to possibilities you never imagined.

Let's take a look at two types of people as it relates to victim thinking.

1. **CREATORS**

    Creators are women and girls who lean in and *create* the life they want. They have thought about and are mindful of where they are today and where they want to go.

2. **WAITERS**

    Waiters are women and girls who wait for life to happen *to* them. They are always responding to things, trying to control and minimize fear, pain, discomfort, and suffering. They react to things rather than taking charge. They expend a lot of energy trying to be small or invisible. External factors influence and control their lives.

Which one could be described as "victim thinking?" The waiters—

those who let life happen to them.

The fact you picked up this book means you probably fall into category No. 1, or you aspire to move from category No. 2 (victim thinking) to category No. 1 (creating the life you want). I applaud you. You will find it much easier to go for your goals when you are making your own choices and not wallowing in the quicksand of perceived powerlessness.

Author Tal Ben-Shahar stated in his book, *Choose the Life You Want: The Mindful Way to Happiness* (2012), that you have to first "choose to choose." In other words, you need to first embrace the fact you have the right and the ability to choose what enters your life and then decide to make choices for yourself every day. It is a state of mind, a personal decision that you can create this world for yourself. Productivity, innovation, and joy are more likely to enter your life when you are in control.

Think for a minute about your friends or the people you have known. To whom are you attracted? Are they negative people who complain about or blame others who "made" them do something or put them in their circumstances? Do they blame others for their lot in life or their inability to do anything now or in the future? These are not the people you want in your life. Negative people attract negative people. Victims attract victims. If you are positive and proactive, you will attract positive people. Likewise, you will find you prefer to be around positive people who energize and support you.

If a friend complains to you over and over, yet never takes steps to remedy a problem, how do *you* feel as the listener? Chances are you feel frustrated and exhausted hearing the broken record of external excuses. Negative people who blame others can be energy pirates who zap the energy out of you. If *you* are an energy pirate, are you attracting healthy people into your life? Probably not. Just think, all your negative energy could be redirected and used proactively to recapture and work on your goals. Whether you identify with using victim thinking yourself or you have friends or family members who fall into that category, be aware and mindful of the negative effects of victim thinking. Recognize it, be mindful of it, and avoid it. Replace negativity with positive words and affirming actions of self-responsibility and power that will help you achieve your goals.

Here are some questions to ask yourself to help determine if you use victim thinking:

1. Have you ever said "I couldn't say anything" about a situation?
2. Have you used words such as he or she "made me do something" or "I had to do something" or "I always have to do something?"
3. Have you found yourself completely blaming someone else for a situation that involved or impacted you?
4. Have you found yourself waiting for someone else to make the first move to get something resolved?
5. Have you ever felt like you don't have a say in a matter that involves you?
6. Have you found yourself putting a lot of energy into complaining about another person's actions or behavior?
7. Are you hesitant, fearful, or don't know how to stand up for yourself?

If you answered yes to any of these questions, you may be stuck thinking you are a victim. It is important to get out of this pattern in order to try new things and realize your personal power. Sorry for the tough love, but you are not a victim unless you choose to be. You are a strong survivor.

Barrier: Lack of Self-Esteem

If you think something is unreachable or not achievable, or that *you* do not *deserve* to be successful or deserve to feel the joy associated with accomplishment, then your self-esteem may need a boost. If you see someone "smarter" than you or who has accomplished "more" than you, how do you react? Do you say, "dang, I need to do more research and try to analyze the steps that person took to reach their goal" so I can reach my goals too? Or, do you retreat and say, "she is just smarter than I am. Achievement would never happen for me," or perhaps just resign yourself to the status quo?

Everyone has times in their life when they question their self-worth or abilities. I know on more than one occasion, I have faced that self-questioning process (e.g., after divorce, conflicts, embarrassing moments, or significant life events). How long you stay in that thinking is what matters.

Pause for a moment. Quietly and mindfully try to identify the self-doubt, self-criticism, and self-judgment you have felt in your life. You may be experiencing it now. Think about the discouraging messages, lasso them together and reorder the words so that they are now positive affirmations. Let compassion, forgiveness, and acceptance rule your mind.

"Success never happens for me."

Replace this thinking with *"Success will happen for me!"*

"I don't deserve my dream."

Replace this thinking with *"I deserve my dream!"*

"I could never reach that goal for myself."

Replace this thinking with *"I can reach that goal!"*

"Good things only happen to other people."

Replace this thinking with *"That can happen to me!"*

"I don't know how to reach my goals."

Replace this thinking with *"I will figure out how to reach my goals!"*

Individually, negative messages you tell yourself can serve as barriers to reaching your goals. Collectively and over time, they can diminish how you feel about yourself. All the messages you give yourself, especially counter-productive ones, impact your self-esteem.

- "I don't feel I have enough talent or skill."
- "Others have success, not me."
- "I'm not disciplined or organized enough."
- "I'm too old."
- "I'm too young."
- "I'm not smart enough."
- "I'm afraid I won't be taken seriously by others."
- "I might be ignored or misunderstood."
- "I might be ridiculed or bullied."
- "Nothing has gone well for me in the past, so why should anything change?"
- "Why bother?"

Additionally, if you absorb and believe these negative messages, you will probably not commit your time, energy, and resources to reach your goals. It creates a cycle of thinking that keeps you stuck so that you never achieve what you want. You must trust and believe in yourself to go for your goals. You are worth the effort! When you stretch yourself and become a little vulnerable (even just a little out of your comfort zone) and then succeed, *that* is how you build self-esteem. Think: stretch and grow. Self-esteem can't grow strong without being stretched. If that statement feels uncomfortable, ask yourself why and explore your answer.

If you have heard yourself making any of the statements above that keep you in the role of victim, think about how you can restructure those words to instead empower yourself.

Remember, you will never rise higher than how you see or visualize yourself. How do you visualize yourself right now?

The activities in PART II will help you look at issues such as self-esteem and help you to begin believing in yourself, your skills, and your goals. I don't even know you, but I believe in you. You are reading this book and you are making an effort to go for the gusto. Good for you! You can do it.

Barrier: Lack of Curiosity

Curiosity is the appetite to learn, the joy of novelty, and the power of exploration. People who are curious have a restless desire for new information or experiences. They view boredom as a negative state to be feverishly avoided.

Curiosity encompasses the capacity to think deeply, beyond the surface. An itch for intellectual and cultural exploration ignite the desire to achieve your goals. Much like travel, curiosity takes you out of yourself as you gain rich access into an idea or topic. From Amelia Earhart to Dora the Explorer, life provides endless opportunities to personally investigate and contemplate.

Curiosity is a response to an information gap. The more you learn, the more you gain knowledge to better adapt to your environment. In that regard, it could be viewed as a Darwinian survival skill.

There are two types of curiosity:

1. Curiosity about how things work (What does a woman entrepreneur need to do to get venture capital?).

2. Curiosity about the thoughts and feelings of others (I wonder why she wanted to start her business?).

Both types of curiosity are valuable to have when pursuing your goals. It gives you a richer picture of how to proceed by looking at things through two levels.

Psychologists use the "Need for Cognition" (NFC) scale to measure intellectual curiosity in men and women. They have found there are ways to distinguish between people who like their mental life to be as stable as possible and others who derive satisfaction and pleasure from the intellectual challenge of curiosity.

Much like the two types of adults we talked about earlier, the waiters and the creators, there are also two types of people regarding curiosity. One type of person obtains just enough information she needs to get by. She does not exert much energy to learn from those around her or from other resources. The second type of person is regularly open to new ideas and experiences. She acts like a sponge, and because of this, she moves ahead and gets more opportunities.

Curiosity is highly correlated with your life situation and environment. Edmund Burke, eighteenth century Irish philosopher, said that curiosity is the first and simplest emotion of the human mind. As children, we ask the adults in our lives to explain new things to us, which is just about everything. If families discourage curiosity ("Stop asking why so much." "You wouldn't understand." "I will tell you when you are older."), children become less curious about their world. Whether a child displays curiosity or not is directly impacted by how the parents responded to the child.

As adults, we are on our own to navigate this complicated world. Those who continue to be curious are more successful survivors and thrivers because they ask a variety of questions, dip their toe into the knowledge pool, and learn things that might benefit them in life. Having a deep bench of knowledge can help you better understand your ever-changing environment. New information, experiences, and insight can also spark a new way of thinking about problems. Curiosity begets resourcefulness, a much-needed skill when going for your goals.

Your life choices can also enhance or quash curiosity. Who you decide to pick as a partner or friend influences whether or not you continue being inquisitive. How supportive is your environment right now with regard to curiosity and openness to new experiences, information and ideas? Curiosity, as well as lack of curiosity, is greatly influenced by your adult environment as well. Incurious people generally experience less pleasure, joy, and creativity than those who are curious.

Shana excelled in math and loved high school. She and her friends cheered at football games, participated in debate tournaments, and played soccer. Shana's senior year was fast approaching, and she began to feel anxious about the big decisions pending in her life—college, gap year, work, or travel. The options sounded both ominous and exciting. She couldn't stop thinking about her aunt who traveled the world, piquing her interest with post cards from exotic locales. Shana regularly looked at those post cards tacked onto her bedroom bulletin board. She visualized herself sitting in a gondola slowly floating in Venetian canals, hiking high in the snow-capped Andes, and strolling through a steamy night market in Cambodia. She also shared the excitement of her math teacher, whose eyes got round like saucers when she described solving difficult calculus problems. But it was her school counselor who recognized Shana's passionate sense of curiosity and encouraged her to channel both of those interests together and apply to a college out of the country. Shana was open to the adventure and did some research on schools. A few months later, Shana found herself flying across the ocean to University of Oxford in England to pursue a math degree.

How do you nurture your curiosity so it helps you reach your goals?

1. **Choose curiosity.** Develop a hungry mind to learn and explore what will make you feel more fulfilled and alive. Don't be afraid to ask questions. Some women don't ask because: (a) They don't want to look stupid (how else will you learn?); or (b) They don't know how to ask. (How do I string the right words together? How do I communicate? What about my accent? Grammar? What are the formal and informal norms about asking questions? Do I raise my hand, interrupt, or blurt out my question?). Look around you. Jump in. You will figure it out.

    When I was in the doctoral program at the University of Oregon, many of my classes had only six to eight students.

Naturally shy, and with my father dying and going through the break-up of my marriage, my self-esteem reached an all-time low. I was oddly quiet. I didn't ask questions or say anything at all unless called upon. Let's just say it was noticeable with so few students in a class. Over time, my self-confidence and curiosity reemerged, reconfigured with a strength that only comes from personal pain and self-reflection (as they say, the harder you fall, the higher you bounce). I look back on that foggy time with mixed feelings and bewilderment. How did I plow through all that? It was hard to manage graduate school, running my business, and moving on alone after a death and breakup. Through it all, curiosity helped me find confidence and the way to reinvent myself.

2. **Be curious about opportunities.** Develop effective strategies and the confidence to recognize opportunities that arise. The more unpredictable the world becomes, the more important it is to remain curious about all opportunities. As you go on this quest to reach your dreams, tapping into your curiosity will help you learn and adapt to the opportunities you may not have considered.

Barrier: Vulnerability

Why is it important to embrace being vulnerable? You may find you feel vulnerable when going for your goals. After all, this is new territory. You may feel alone or a little insecure. Vulnerability, a willingness to do or try something with no guarantee of outcome, is the foundation for personal growth. You grow and gain confidence with each step you take. Feeling this way can bring joy, innovation, and creativity. In other words, being vulnerable is a necessary building block for reaching your goals.

Dr. Brené Brown (2010), an author and researcher on vulnerability and shame, found that women who have a sense of worthiness are more likely and willing to be vulnerable. They do not see vulnerability as a weakness but rather synonymous with courage. They develop the strength and grit to be imperfect and to love themselves. They lean into the discomfort of vulnerability with mindfulness and determination.

Brown's research also found that you can't ignore specific uncomfortable emotions associated with vulnerability. When you try to numb (aka ignore) yourself with alcohol, drugs, overeating, compulsive shopping, gambling, and the like, you numb all emotions, including happiness and joy. You lose touch with your authentic self and the direction of the path to your dreams.

Barrier: Impatience

We are a society of instant gratification. Email is too slow, so we text; ovens are too slow, so we microwave. We download and upload. We prioritize speed. How patient will you be when you pursue your goals? For example, maybe you can't wait four years to finish college, or the months it takes to save money for a car, or the years of practice to be a good musician. You get frustrated because your rewards don't come fast enough, so you take shortcuts (like getting unreasonable loans, extending yourself too far, dropping out of school), or you modify your dreams or simply let your dreams die. Dream drain! A dream—*your* dream—is good enough to wait for. Be patient and steadfast.

I had a college roommate who used to say, "Patience is a virtue, virtue is a grace; put them both together and you have a happy face!" Okay, she may have been just a little too perky and cheerful, especially around exam time, but I've got to give it to her. She was always patient, calm and positive.

Barrier: Scarcity

Researchers Sendhil Mullainatham, a Harvard economist, and Eldar Shafir, a Princeton psychologist, found that when you are lacking something significant in your life that affects your well-being (such as money, food, love, companionship, time), you tend to over-focus on that thing (Mullainatham and Shafir 2013). This scarcity mindset creates tunnel vision which can lead to bad choices. A scarcity mindset may help you manage your immediate day-to-day world, but other skills and abilities (such as attention, mindfulness, self-control, and long-term planning) often suffer.

Thinking that you are lacking something in your life can create huge psychic consequences, distorting how you think and stifling your capability to achieve balance. Short-term decisions based on real or perceived scarcity can dig you deeper into a negative situation (e.g., more in debt by overusing your credit card, hanging onto toxic relationships, questioning whether you can survive without a man) because you don't look at the big picture. The scarcity trap causes you to lose sight of long-term priorities which can often make your problems worse.

The ability to recognize what feels scarce to you right now allows you to take steps to prevent harmful consequences. Identify how much attention and energy you are giving this feeling, try to create more balance, look up from the immediate field of awareness, and look out to your long-term goals. Once you know how scarcity affects your daily life, you can manage its effects more competently.

Barrier: Multi-Tasking

We all have a love-hate relationship with multitasking—doing many things at the same time. Some people seem able to handle multiple tasks concurrently, but for many, the challenge can lead to not doing anything well. Multitasking can also interfere with mindfully seeking your goals. Juggling too much can distract your attention and consume your time. Multitasking can reduce efficiency and performance because your brain can only focus on one thing at a time. Researchers at Stanford University found that undertaking many tasks at once can be less productive than doing a single thing at a time. Some multitaskers have more trouble organizing their thoughts and filtering out irrelevant information.

Therefore, because of our crazy, multitasking electronic life, remember to carve out time to concentrate and be present with your goals.

Women in general try to balance more demands in their lives than men. Research suggests that, because women have more synapses between different parts of the brain than their male counterPARTs, these connections helped women to survive in evolutionary terms. In the home, women kept the fire stoked, the house safe and clean, crying children tended to, and saber-toothed tigers at bay. Women had, and continue to have, a lot to juggle in their daily lives. Even today, with most homes in the United States having two breadwinners, women who work outside the home still do the majority of the housework such as cleaning, cooking, laundry, shopping, and child care. Think about all the tasks you try to manage. Identify which of those juggling balls suspended in the air you can put down long enough to enjoy quality time with just you and your dreams.

Barrier: Feeling Unlucky

Some people believe it just takes luck for your dreams to come true. You have probably known someone who seems to have all the luck. Things always go her way. But is that accurate? There may be another perspective on all that luck she seems to possess.

English writer Abi Oborne (2016) wrote an interesting article in the *Huffington Post* titled, *My Husband: Five Reasons I Am Not Lucky to Have Him.* Her premise was that luck had nothing to do with her marital relationship. One day, someone observed her husband changing their baby's diaper and told her she was lucky to have a husband who did that. She responded that she and her husband had decided to have children together; raising children is not *her* job, it is *their* job. She chose her husband based on many factors using her brain not dice. To say she is lucky implies that all women must let life *happen* to them with no voice or control and just accept the luck of the draw. Women who accept their worth, equality, and the value of their own voice make things happen. Oborne and her husband found and chose each other. The author makes a strong argument that life is a series of everyday choices with very little *luck* involved.

So, luck doesn't just happen. *You* play a significant role in facilitating favorable circumstances to enter your life.

To have a successful outcome of any kind, five factors are necessary, only one of which is luck:

1. You know what you want.

2. You look for opportunities (which will be easier to spot when you know what you want).

3. You are ready and prepared to seize these opportunities (which are more likely to happen if you think about this ahead of time).

4. You embrace the wise words of Nike—Just do it! —dare to begin, and act upon the opportunity.

5. The wild card is luck itself, being in the right place at the right time with all the factors perfectly aligned (e.g., weather, finances, health, seat mate on the airplane). Without putting energy in STEPS 1 to 4, the "luck" in STEP 5 would probably just fade away.

Now that we understand how luck doesn't just happen by itself, let's explore the concepts of wishing and dreaming. There is a difference between having a wish and a dream. A wish has more of an ephemeral, magical quality. You wait to see if it happens or not. You blow out those birthday candles and operators are standing by. A dream, on the other hand, is more like a goal. It has possibilities and actions behind it. You are taking charge and in control. Your hands are on the steering wheel of the road of life, making your dreams happen. A wish is passive, and a dream is active.

Where do you want to place your wager? On luck and wishing? Or would you prefer to take active steps to reach your dreams?

Barrier: Unrealistic Expectations versus Dreaming Big

Dream big! Why not? It takes the same energy to dream big as it does to dream small. You are fortunate to live in a world where many societal barriers for women have been reduced, opening up a world of possibilities.

Not that long ago, women and girls who pursued their goals were viewed as "not very ladylike." Nowadays, our culture approves of women wanting to be a doctor (when being a nurse was the only medical occupation for women a few years ago) or an astronaut (when women could only be on terra firma in a clerical position in the past). You can be a president, or mechanic, a scientist, a firefighter, an Olympic athlete, a pilot, a commercial fisher, or a mother. If the women before us had not dreamed big, these opportunities would not be available for the rest of us today.

Disabilities or life circumstances need not stop you from dreaming big. One of my friends is dyslexic and never had children. She went on to get her Ph.D. and now works as a national expert in child development. She persisted, was passionate, and knew she could do it. There are so many stories of the athletes or the Oprahs in the world who have defied the odds with hard work and an internal fire that kept them dreaming and moving towards their goals. They are all inspirational.

Barrier: Procrastination

My favorite quote about procrastination is taped near my computer so I see it every day:

> *"Be decisive. Right or wrong, make a decision. The road of life is paved with flat squirrels who couldn't decide."*
> UNKNOWN AUTHOR

We've all been there. We start out with good intentions, great energy, and maybe even a plan. Yet, the project never gets off the ground. The goal is never reached. We feel deflated.

There are many reasons why women and girls procrastinate. One of the main reasons, once again, is fear. But procrastination can also disguise itself in other ways, such as withdrawing socially or engaging in over-activity. Do you find yourself running here and there to appointments, lessons, sports, home, work, and seemingly endless other places? Do you find you have no downtime? Do you feel like you are competing for the title of Super-mom, Super-friend, or Super-student of the Year? You may give the appearance you are just too busy to get to the task at hand, while in fact you have created the busyness to avoid the task. Once you think about and address these fears and evasive behaviors, you will find you procrastinate less often. Once again, if your goal is a priority, you will find the time.

Another cause of procrastination is poor time management, which we will talk about separately in more detail. However, start thinking about procrastination and its relationship to time for you. How do you typically achieve things large and small? Do you just let your day unfold and squeeze as much in as you can? Do you make regular to-do lists to organize your time and prioritize those tasks? If so, are they daily, weekly, or monthly lists, and how specific are they? How influential and respectful are others in your world, regarding your to-do lists and goals? How effective is your get-things-done style? Are you happy with it? Is it getting you to your goals? Why do you think you have not yet achieved your goals? Why do you think you are taking longer to achieve these goals than you'd like?

We all procrastinate. As a writer, I often hear colleagues say, "I'm just not motivated to write, so I haven't been at the computer for weeks." Or I might hear a friend say, "I need to sort those old family photos, but I just can't inspire myself to do it." Procrastinators often have it backwards. They think they need to be motivated, driven, uber-caffeinated, or energized first before tackling their goal. In fact, doing the action first (e.g., sorting the photos) often generates the inspiration. Jumping in, even without your mental energy, may be helpful to move you along.

Procrastination is motivation's evil twin. If you can't get going or make progress towards your goal, try following these six anti-procrastination steps:

1. **Drill Down.** Be mindful of what is going on with you when you get stuck. At that point, drill deeply by asking yourself the "why" questions. Why do I feel stuck? (Then answer.)

Next, ask yourself "why" to that answer. Then ask "why" to that answer. Keep asking why until you begin to get to the heart of the issue.

2. **Chunk It!** Chunk the steps or tasks into smaller units to get to your goal. It might feel less overwhelming. Even if you have a small dream and you fulfill it (e.g., go by myself to Yellowstone Park, a play, a yoga retreat, a class), you will gain confidence in your achievement. You will probably find yourself saying, "Hey, I can do this! Now, I can go do the next step (or go for another dream)!"

3. **Find Support.** Work with a partner, coach, friend, or colleague. Find a goal soulmate who will help keep you on track and be your cheerleader.

4. **Stir Up Passion and Drive.** Regularly revisit your goal, your passion for that goal, and whether it's still a fit for you. We will talk more about this in PART II in relation to your Goal Objects.

5. **Be Mindful of Your Barriers.** As Elizabeth Gilbert talks about in her book, *Big Magic,* look your barriers in the face, put them in the back seat of your car where you can keep an eye on them, don't let them touch the steering wheel, and keep driving down the road you have selected. Great metaphor!

6. **Be Mindful of Your Skills.** Give yourself a pat on the back and a pep talk. Talk to yourself as you would a friend. Remind yourself of all your great qualities and skills to make your dreams come to fruition.

The point with procrastination, as with motivation, is to be mindful and honest with yourself. If you do the six steps above, you will be able to see what is going on for you. If you can identify procrastination, you can manage it.

Barrier: Negative Feelings about Not Pursuing Your Dreams in the Past

Some women and girls feel self-loathing, jealousy, or bitterness deep down because at some time in their lives, they stopped pursuing their dreams. Unless dealt with, these feelings bubble out in passive-aggressive ways, negative and hurtful indirect communication, health problems, drama, and/or anger. The behaviors can be directed inward as well as outward towards loved ones. These petty drips of inner hostility can become waterfalls.

Dreams rarely go away. When they are repressed or prematurely dismissed, resentment can creep in without your even knowing it. Perhaps you used to love to sing, but stopped taking choir classes because your high school boyfriend (who is now history) wanted more of your time. Maybe when you got married, you stopped dancing. Maybe your peers used to call you a nerd because you were a girl and good at computers. (You could have given Bill Gates a run for his money!) Some women hand over their power and wait to be rescued by Prince Charming. (Thank you, Walt Disney, for this image that has messed with our minds.) Okay, maybe Mr. Charming did gallantly rescue you to live happily ever after. How did that work for you? By its very definition, being rescued means giving your power over to someone else. Dream drain! After the rescue, did you stop thinking about your dreams? Probably not.

When your dreams have never been fulfilled or actualized, they rarely go away, whether or not there is a galloping white horse, pumpkin carriage, or castle with a stunning view.

Overly strong attachments to someone (like your rescuer) can cause you to feel imbalanced and lose clarity of thought about many things, including your goals and dreams. Clinging and grasping to someone else, or to a fantasy, distracts you from your goals. This behavior can blind you. When you believe in and control your own power and abilities, you loosen that tight grip. You also become a healthier, equal partner. As you let go, you awaken to the world and to wonderful opportunities and possibilities.

Carnie met Adam, the love of her life, her junior year in high school. He proposed on the shore of nearby Watson Lake one warm summer evening. Carnie later bragged to friends that "I caught him." (They assumed this reference was to Adam and not the fish in the lake.) The friends smiled but found her expression odd.

When they both turned twenty-one, the lovebirds had a large Catholic wedding. Neither of them had really ever dated others, nor lived on their own. Carnie moved directly from her parent's house to the small apartment she and her new husband rented above a downtown coffee shop.

Their codependence started with little things. Carnie did not know what to do when a ceiling light went out or the TV screen went blank. The dishwasher flooded and, instead of turning off the water valve or calling the landlord, she stuffed all the towels and clothes she could find along the floorboard and waited until her husband came home from work five hours later.

Carnie became pregnant the year after she married Adam. She began feeling more and more isolated and bored. Her husband spent long hours repairing electrical lines after storms and occasionally going out with his buddies after work. She began to blame him for her unhappiness. Since she had been a little girl, all she wanted was to find a man and be married. She thought having a husband would fulfill her. He would define her and make her complete. Her world would revolve around him. After some serious soul-searching and growing up, Carnie realized only *she* could make herself happy. She acknowledged she didn't know who she was or what she wanted. She felt numb, unable to reach down inside herself to find what made her happy or what she wanted out of life.

Negative feelings can emerge due to unrealized dreams. They also appear because, as females, we can be pretty hard on ourselves. Negative feelings often manifest themselves as indifference, depression, physical ailments (e.g., headaches, digestive problems, high blood pressure), difficulty sticking to one thing/follow through, shame, self-pity, or guilt. Explore these things, if you experience them, to understand the cause. The goal is not to get angry or fill your life with regret, but rather to take any negative energy, learn from it, and redirect it down the path of your choosing. At the end of this path you will not only capture your goals and dreams but reclaim a confident, positive attitude as well.

Do any of these barriers sound familiar to you? The experience of creating your own GO! display will allow you to recapture those lost dreams and feel more positive and in control of your destiny. The goals and dreams symbolized in your display are yours. You now know they aren't your parents' dreams. They aren't your partner's dreams. They aren't Prince Charming's dreams. They are your own dreams. You own them and can protect them. No one else can make them happen or take them away. This realization can be life changing.

The obstacles we have talked about in this chapter may feel a bit overwhelming and insurmountable. However, looking inward, asking yourself tough questions, and being mindful of these barriers is half the battle. Staying upbeat and positive also helps. Researchers have found that pessimists are more likely to view life's roadblocks as personal and permanent. Optimists look at roadblocks as temporary, expected, and navigable.

CHAPTER 7

Visualization with Goal Objects

We have covered the foundational information about pursuing your goals and identifying your barriers. Now we are ready for action—exploring how visualizing your dreams using Goal Objects can serve as a powerful tool in capturing your goals.

Objects you select and group into one spot, into a GO! area, take on their own unique energy and clarity. Objects symbolizing your goals don't just tell any story, they tell *your* story. When looked at every day, these ordinary objects can help you visualize goals and allow new opportunities into your life.

The Goal Objects are not only a collection of items that represent your goals, they are also objects that represent the support and resources in your life that will help you reach those goals (tangible things as well as people who inspire and encourage you).

Creating this special space with meaningful objects is a deeply personal journey. The process becomes an exploration of what feeds you and gives you joy and fulfillment, awakening energy and ideas. The Goal Objects can be fanciful or serious, intricate or simple. You are creating a GO! display just for you. You can choose whatever objects you want to put into your container or tabletop display.

The grouping of Goal Objects becomes a place to pause, be introspective, and think about the symbolism of the objects in front of you. This physical reminder plays the role of a compass, keeping you on track in the direction you have chosen, by regularly reminding you of your goals.

THE POWER OF VISUALIZATION AND GOAL OBJECTS

Objects stimulate visualization. Visualization stimulates thought. Thoughts stimulate words. Words stimulate actions. So, if you change your visualization, you can change your life!

Research suggests that visualization impacts how the brain functions. Brain neurons (cells that transmit information) interpret over time an image such as a Goal Object similar to a real-life situation requiring an action. The brain generates an impulse that tells neurons to do the action. The image creates a new neural pathway, clusters of cells that prepare the body to do actions consistent with what was being imagined through visualization. Visualization keeps a person linked to their goal, thus increasing their chances of seizing that goal. That vivid mental snapshot keeps you going when inevitable roadblocks appear.

Top athletes have long practiced visualization as a way to stay focused on their tasks and to reach their goals. They close their eyes and *imagine* the field, course, or track and see themselves making a goal, diving off the high board into the pool, or jumping all the hurdles. They also visualize themselves being a winner on the awards' stand, bending forward and getting that shiny gold metal placed around their neck. Visualizing yourself as a pro tennis player, going to college, losing weight, starting a business, traveling to India, or learning to play the piano are powerful images. Everything begins to feel like it is within reach and doable.

I'm sure you have heard the old adage by Benjamin Franklin, "If you fail to plan, you are planning to fail." The power of planning and goal setting is evident in much of the business and self-help literature. Yet, regularly *visualizing and focusing* on your personal or professional goals is often overlooked. Not only is it just as important to visualize and focus, these steps are essential to success. Mindfulness, visualization, and focus form a powerful tool for women and girls seeking their goals.

You have to participate fearlessly and passionately in the planning and manifestation of your own goals. It is an ongoing process to grow and live your best life. Are you ready for the four steps to create your GO! display and reach your goals? Turn the page and let's get started!

PART II

Four Easy Steps to Reaching Your Goals

THE FOUR STEPS

"There is no force more powerful than a woman determined to rise"

W. E. B. DUBOIS

Creating your own collection of Goal Objects is not just about the final product. Much of what you will learn is embedded in the four steps to get there. Step-by-step, you will build your own GO! display while gaining insight into yourself. You will have an opportunity to dig deeper into your own life, identify what feeds your soul, and determine what motivates and inspires you. You will learn to recognize the positive influences around you, become clearer about your goals and dreams, gain the confidence to reach your full potential and achieve what you set forth to do. It is important to trust the process and be open to what you learn.

The objectives of the four steps are:

STEP 1: Identify your goals and dreams.

STEP 2: Collect the objects you want to put in your GO! display that represents your goals. Find a container for the objects. Understand the symbolism of each object and different kinds of containers.

STEP 3: Decorate your GO! container. Place the objects in the container. Find an appropriate location for the GO! display.

STEP 4: Develop your goal Action Plan. Create a ritual or routine at your GO! display to help you visualize and focus.

I developed these four steps because it provided a linear structure to help a person move forward through the process. It is difficult to start collecting objects if you aren't clear about your dreams and goals. It is challenging to find a container until you know what objects you have to put into it. Each step builds upon the previous step, guiding you to your goal.

Ready? First, select a comfortable setting as you work through the four steps. Create a quiet space with minimal interruptions. Step away from your cell phone, television, and other distractions. Think about what type of environment will work for you as you go through the process. Some women and girls like a cozy chair to sit in, soothing music to listen to and a cup of tea or hot chocolate to sip. You may also want to light a candle to create a feeling of comfort and calm. This can help you slow down and focus. Sit quietly for a couple of minutes to relax and unwind. Take a few deep breaths and be attentive to this time you have set aside for yourself. When you feel relaxed and ready, read this inspirational thought:

> *Keep your dreams alive. Understand to achieve anything*
> *requires faith and belief in yourself, vision, hard work,*
> *determination, and dedication. Remember all things*
> *are possible for those who believe.*
> GAIL DEVERS

As you begin this process, make a commitment to yourself to do self-care along the way. The creative process is fun and exciting, but it can be emotionally taxing as well. Give yourself permission to be human. Going for your goals is not a straight line. Expect cheers and tears. So, raise your right hand and agree to get some exercise, allow for adequate sleep, eat healthy foods, and talk out issues and emotions that arise.

Pampering yourself is also encouraged: a bubble bath, quiet time, gentleness, being in nature—whatever is a treat for you.

STEP 1

Identifying Your Goals and Dreams

> ### Step 1: Objectives
> 1. Identify your goals and dreams
> 2. Gain an understanding of your motivations, support system and both internal and external barriers. Learn how to tackle your fears and barriers.

What Are Your Goals and Dreams?

Let's start this first step by doing an exercise that gets at the heart of how you feel about your goals and dreams and what you want to discover.

Letter to Myself

Date _____

Dear _____ ,

As I begin this process to pursue my goals and dreams, I feel:

_____
_____
_____
_____

I want to discover about myself:

_____
_____
_____
_____

Love,

_____

Look back at this letter from time to time to measure your progress and how your feelings and expectations have changed.

Ask yourself this basic question: What do I want to do with my life? Answering this isn't easy for many people. If you ask a child what she wants to be when she grows up, most are quick to give you an answer. "I want to be a teacher." "I want to be a ballerina." "I want to travel to exotic lands in a hot air balloon." Think back to when you were a child and the world was your oyster. You probably weren't even aware of any reason why all your dreams wouldn't come true.

I remember going to summer camp as a child and on the last night of camp, all the girls gathered around Lake Kilowan with our "dream boats." Although that name might sound like a code word for George Clooney, they were actual boats made of bark, moss, macaroni letters, and meaningful trinkets. We ceremoniously lit the candle in the middle of the boat, made a wish, and with anticipatory zeal, pushed the dream boat out into the lake to begin its magical journey. We believed that our wishes would then come true (assuming the moss didn't catch on fire first).

Let's get the memory juices flowing by writing down your dreams from your childhood.

Dreams From My Childhood

When you were a little girl, what did you dream about doing or being when you grew up (a job you wanted, an adventure to go on, a location you wanted to live, the places you wanted to travel, skills to learn, sports to play)?

_____
_____
_____
_____

Did you experience dream drain? What happened to that dream?

_____
_____

Do you want to revive that dream? Why or why not?

_____
_____
_____

You received many messages growing up. Powerful messages conveyed through words and actions generally come from our family of origin (mothers, fathers, relatives), or teachers and others who influenced us. These messages could have been positive or negative statements about your value or self-worth. They could have been messages about your goals. When you are young, all messages are formative.

Messages impact your view of the world and the image you have of yourself. They emerge throughout life in both healthy and unhealthy ways. The good news is that, with a little work, these messages can be changed. First, you must identify the messages that are harmful or counterproductive. Then replace them with positive affirmations and experiences that give you a better foundation to then move towards your goals. The following activity will help you identify your early messages.

Early Messages

As a child, my mother would tell me _____

    I felt _____ after that.

As a child, my father would tell me _____

    I felt _____ after that.

As a child, my teacher(s) would tell me _____

    I felt _____ after that.

The one thing I would hear as a child that deflated my dreams was _____

I grew up thinking successful girls/women were described as _____

If someone said I was smart or had talent, I thought they _____

The person(s) who believed in me was _____

He/she would tell me _____

Good job. Now let's dig a little deeper into those childhood messages and see how they can affect dream drain and the pursuit of your goals well into adulthood. As we talked about in PART I, being curious is an important skill to have in order to stay sharp, make informed decisions, and reach your goals. So, how curious are you?

Curiosity

Put an "x" in the boxes that describe you at different points in your life.

MY CURIOSITY AS A...	VERY CURIOUS	SOMEWHAT CURIOUS	AVERAGE CURIOSITY	SOMEWHAT INCURIOUS	NOT CURIOUS
CHILD					
TEEN					
ADULT					

If your curiosity has waned over the years, why do you think that occurred?

_____
_____
_____

Give an example of something about which you were curious but discouraged to explore?

_____
_____
_____

Give an example of something about which you were curious and were encouraged to explore?

_____
_____
_____

Now that you have identified your childhood dreams, early messages you received as a child, as well as how your curiosity was fostered, let's shift gears to the present. Without editing or judgement, write down your thoughts. Ask yourself: What do I want for myself *right* now?

What Do I Want For Myself?

What do you want most?

What kind of life do you dream about having?

Are you living the life you want? What do you want to change or be different?

What brings you joy and makes you feel alive? What experiences have you had that felt the happiest and most free?

What experiences and accomplishments do you want to have?

If you are young and your whole life is ahead of you, how do you want to fill it?

If you are trying to be a present/mindful mom with your children, how do you juggle that role and still pursue your goals?

If you are winding down your career, what do you want the next chapter of your life to look like?

What is on your bucket list (things you want to do before you "kick the bucket")?

If failure was not an option and you could do anything, what would that be?

If you were looking back five to ten years from now, what would you like to say you accomplished?

What future regret(s) would you have if you had not done or tried to do something now?

What would you like your legacy to be?

Another way to home in on what you want in life is to write as fast as you can about your dreams without editing or censoring. This exercise should help you get to your core interests and desires.

I Wish / I Want

I wish / I want: _____

I wish / I want: _____

I wish / I want: _____

I wish / I want: _____

I wish / I want: _____

I wish / I want: _____

I wish / I want: _____

I wish / I want: _____

I wish / I want: _____

I wish / I want: _____

I wish / I want: _____

Your goals are more likely to come to fruition if they are tangible and specific. Additionally, goals need to be understandable, measurable, and within a time frame. Therefore, try to be concrete when you identify your goals: I want a horse by the time I turn twenty-four. I want to work as a doctor in Uganda before I start a family. I want to be a professional soccer player after college. I want to open my own food truck next year using our old family recipes. I want to buy a house in Montana when I retire. I want to visit my grandchildren three times a year.

As you narrow down your dreams into concrete goals, try to avoid vague references. For example, in your goal statements, rather than saying, "I want to travel," instead say, "I want to go to Kenya on a photographic safari within the next five years." Avoid terms like less, more, reduce, or increase in your goal statement. Establish actual numbers, locations, steps, or tasks. For instance, a phrase such as, "be a kinder person" is not as clear and powerful as, "tell my mother I love her every time we talk on the phone" or "write a letter to Grandma once a month." What does a goal of "be less shy" or "be more confident" mean? Instead, use specific action words such as "join Toastmasters Club in March," or "firmly shake my boss's hand next time I see him/her." What does "be less fearful and risk averse" mean? Instead, say, "learn to scuba dive this summer" or "drive by myself in May to the Rock and Roll Hall of Fame in Cincinnati."

If your dream revolves around obtaining money, ask yourself if there is an emotion you are trying to feel or satisfy (e.g., security, happiness, power, respect, importance, value)? What is your relationship with money? There is nothing inherently wrong with wanting money, but a dream solely based on accumulating wealth will often leave a person feeling empty.

Ask yourself if your goal is a passing fancy, or if it is a long-term aspiration. You can have both, but don't be afraid to dream big and long-term.

In the next activity, you will write down your short-term and long-term goals. Refer back to the rapid-fire "I wish/I want" activity you just completed for ideas. Your goals can be personal, professional, or both. Write quickly about whatever comes to mind from your heart. Don't judge yourself, edit, or censor at this point. This is just for you unless you want to share it with others. Stretch yourself. The free-flowing ideas you write down are often the best fit.

What Are My Short- and Long-Term Goals?

Short-term goals:

Long-term goals:

How do you feel after doing this activity? Do you feel joy? Excitement? Happiness? Amazement? Anticipation? Eagerness? Passion? Confidence? Or do you feel sadness? Fear? Trepidation? Confusion? Insecurity? Exploring these emotions can help point you to the right path so these feelings don't reemerge as a barrier or roadblock later.

If you are on an authentic, mindful path to your goals, you will feel passionate and excited about the journey. Consequently, what you do to get there won't feel like a burden or sacrifice. Rather, steps towards your goal will bring satisfaction. Look back at your list and put a star next to the short- and long-term goals that give you a feeling of joy.

In one week, come back to this activity. Has anything changed? Do you feel the same? Is there anything you would add or delete? Would you move or change any of the stars you put next to your joyful goals? Do you feel some comfort now where there was previously fear or vice versa? Continue digging a little deeper to mine more personal goals. Keep adding things to this list as you work through the exercise. Be mindful of all your feelings as you collect your Goal Objects and create your display.

The Motivation Behind Your Dreams

In PART I, we talked about motivation. What are the motivations behind your goals? You are more likely to reach your goals and enjoy the experience along the way if your motivation is positive, such as having a desire to succeed, have fun, or challenge yourself. Negative motivators are less helpful in propelling you forward. For example, negative motivators might include wanting to get even or take revenge, to cause harm to someone else, to put someone down, to exercise power over someone through competition, or to take resources from another person. These motivations rarely enable healthy goal-seeking. Take some time to explore why you selected your particular goals.

Do you want _____

- Glory and fame
- Wealth
- Prestige
- Security – financial and emotional
- Safety
- Validation from others
- Sense of accomplishment
- Personal growth
- Competition
- Good health
- Sense of belonging
- Spiritual enrichment
- Joy and happiness

Are you trying to prove yourself to **someone else** or do you want to improve yourself for yourself?

What Are the Motivations or Reasons Behind My Goal(s)?

Setting up little rewards or motivators for yourself along the way can be helpful, especially when going for long-term goals. These rewards might include doing something special for yourself, such as getting a manicure, shopping for new clothes, going out to eat, or going to the beach.

How much time (daily, monthly, yearly) are you willing to devote to making your dreams come true? Do you need more information to help you plan out a timeline? Are you prepared and committed to invest this time? If not, why aren't you? Do you divide your activities into smaller, more manageable steps so you can see progress more often? What is the best way for you to be successful and keep to the timeline you have set for yourself?

> **My Goal Timeline**
>
> How long will it take to reach your goals (sketch out the steps on a timeline)?
>
> How do you feel about the amount of time it will take to reach your goals? How would you describe your level of commitment to this timeline?

A timeline is a map to guide and propel you forward. As you proceed, if you find yourself wanting to give up on a goal, replace it with another goal. Don't completely throw in the towel. Rethink or reconfigure the goal and strategize about what those new steps would look like. Midcourse adjustments are normal and expected. This is an organic process. Your dreams may shift or change a few times before you are even done with the process. These adjustments show you are organic and growing too. The result will be goals that are well thought-out, compatible, and moving at a comfortable pace.

Who or What Supports Your Dreams?

Great things are rarely accomplished alone. Think about all the things that support you every day in pursuit of your dreams and goals. We all have varying degrees of resources around us. Some we use and some we ignore. Resources may cover our basic needs such as food and shelter. They may also include money, time, space, opportunities, knowledge, skills, or abilities. Some of these resources are tangible, and others intangible. Some are internal (skills you have), while some are external to you (assistance and influences).

You have probably thought about the resources you need to reach your goals. Resources can be things like working space or office space, time, money, energy, social support, child care, or training. Resources can also include services from a mentor, pet sitter, lawyer, personal trainer, carpenter, accountant, or computer technician. Your list is specific to your goal. Almost everyone lists money as their top priority. As a word of caution, money can be an artificial barrier and cause you to feel stuck if it doesn't materialize. I encourage you to use creative thinking regarding money. There are often innovative ways to achieve your goals without much money, such as trading services, starting smaller, buying used equipment, and similar strategies.

Resources I Need to Reach My Goals

What are the resources you need to reach your dreams and goals?

What are the resources around you?

What resources do you need to create, cultivate, or find?

How might you obtain or access those needed resources?

In PART I, we talked about who supports you in your dreams, goals, and ambitions. If that is a difficult question to answer, reflect on the people in your life. Some people make you feel good and others do not.

Supportive people are good listeners. They may be mentors who have accomplished a similar dream, creative thinkers, people who are encouraging and kind, or helpers who share tasks so you can work towards your dream. They could include teachers, neighbors, parents, siblings, friends, or relatives. You might find encouragement through a supervisor or coworker. Supportive friends may be in your book club, church, or bird-watching group. Take a look around your world. Some people may have one significant, positive person in their lives, while others may have several.

Do the people around you look out for your best interests? What do these people do or say? Supportive people use phrases such as:

Go for it!

That is great (cool, awesome, amazing, wonderful).

You'd be excellent for that.

I admire your vision.

Why not give it a try?

Life is short.

Good for you.

What do you want?

How can I help and support you to reach your goal?

Identify people who make you feel positive about yourself, give honest feedback, and show support.

Supportive People Around Me

Who are the people around you that support your dreams?

Does it feel healthy to be around these people (e.g., you're free from negative comments, put-downs, competition, or jealousy)?

In what way(s) do they or can they support you in your quest for your dreams?

How can you develop your own inner cheerleader if these people are not around?

It takes a lot of courage to show your dreams to someone else.
ERMA BOMBECK

What happens to your spirit and dreams when you are around negative people? How does your body feel when you spend time with pessimistic, emotionally unhealthy, or toxic people who don't support you? Compare that to how you feel when you are around positive people.

Toxic / Negative People Around Me

Who are toxic/negative people in your life?

What are the behavioral signs or red flags that identify people who don't support you?

How can I avoid being around these negative people?

My mother was a loving, wonderful woman. Yet she was protective and not much of a risk-taker. I can't fault her. She was a product of her upbringing during an era when the role of women was quite prescribed. To my ears, her motherly comments at times felt discouraging, even though her motivation wasn't at all mean-spirited. I knew she took pride in me and I would in no way give her the label of negative or toxic. Yet every so often, she would show restraint about something I wanted to pursue, either by saying nothing or by cautioning, "I just don't want you to be disappointed if it doesn't work out." The risk of my disappointment seemed to carry more weight than the potential of my feeling joy and a sense of accomplishment. Of course, I understood that she was just trying to protect me and that she saw things from the lens of her world. With that awareness in hand, while valuing her wisdom and love, I had to blaze my own trail. I learned that her ability to support had its limits in the context of my pursuing certain goals, and that was okay. She supported me in many other loving ways. I sought out other people more in my work world who could provide that sounding board and the cheerleading I needed in that context.

Some people in your world may laugh or make fun of you and your dreams. Others may be cruel, question you, or simply not be the right fit to understand and support your dreams. Be conscious and mindful of these people and the things they do that make you feel discouraged. Exercise the personal power you have to move away from them. They aren't helping, are they?

> *Keep away from people who try to belittle your ambitions.*
> *Small people always do that, but the really great make you*
> *feel that you too can become great.*
> MARK TWAIN

Now that you have identified the supportive and less supportive people in your life, what do you do next? Look at the activities you just completed. Think about all the resources you indicated that you need to reach your goals. Next, look at the list you made of positive people in your life. Now, match up those two lists. Is there anyone on the positive-people list who could help you with the resources you need? Have you shared your dreams and goals with these supportive people? How do they support your dreams now? How might they support your dreams in the future?

Feel free to reach out and talk to your supporters. Don't hesitate to ask them for assistance. Share your ideas and seek referrals from them. This kind of networking forms the core of most successful endeavors. Also, use these supporters to get feedback about your goals and strategies. Engage your supportive friends and family to help you think of creative ways to realize your dreams. If that beach house you dreamt about exceeds your means, maybe you can purchase it with friends, rather than on your own, so you only pay a percentage of the cost. Perhaps you can write your great novel at a friend's mountain cabin in exchange for child care. Maybe someone will watch your own kids while you take time to work on your goals.

Once you get your resources and supports in line, you are one step closer to reaching your goals.

Role Models

Who are the people you admire? Whose lives do you aspire to emulate? Who are your role models? Perhaps someone you watched on TV or read about doing great things inspired you to say, "I want to do that!" Your role models might include just one person or a range of individuals, such as: Harriet Tubman, Mahatma Gandhi, Martin Luther King, Jr., Oprah Winfrey, Eleanor Roosevelt, Mother Teresa, Joan Baez, or Princess Diana. How do these role models relate to your dreams and aspirations? What parts of their lives do you admire? You may want to put objects, such as a picture or symbol, in your GO! display that represents your role models.

My Role Models

Who are your role models?

Why do you admire them?

Your Environment

Your environment can affect your ability to be creative and how big you dream. Identify the type of surroundings that work well for you. What energizes you? What drives you crazy? What helps you concentrate? What disrupts your planning or creativity? For example, from time to time, I go on solitary retreats where I take my easel pad and colored markers to a rented place at the beach. More often, I just hole up in my home basement office or go to a coffee shop to brainstorm with a blank book and decaf nonfat latte. I schedule the time in my calendar and honor the commitment to myself. It feels special, like a retreat, and I get a lot accomplished.

Dreaming Big

Describe the environment or situation that allows you to dream big. It could be a physical setting or set of circumstances.

How can you create that environment for yourself?

Barriers to Dreaming Big

In PART I, we talked about common roadblocks and barriers women and girls face when pursuing their goals. Now let's take a look at the specific challenges you may be facing. In the activity below, circle all the barriers or obstacles that apply to you in your life. Put a star by those things you want to try to change. You will refer to this list throughout this chapter.

Barriers in My Life

Circle all that apply. Put a star next to the barriers you want to work on or change.

- Time, Energy and Planning
- Fear of Failure
- Fear of Success
- Fear of Being Different
- Perfectionism
- Self-Sabotage
- Sabotage by Others
- Trauma
- Learned Helplessness – Victim Thinking
- Lack of Self-Esteem
- Lack of Curiosity
- Vulnerability
- Impatience
- Feelings of Scarcity
- Multi-tasking
- Feeling Unlucky
- Unrealistic Expectations vs. Dreaming Big
- Procrastination
- Negative Feelings from the Past

Other: _____

_____

_____

Internal Barriers

Barriers can either be internal or external. By recognizing both kinds of barriers, you can more easily develop strategies to get around them or deal with them. Let's start by looking at internal barriers—those messages you tell yourself about what you should and should not do to reach your goals as well as your behaviors that may hinder your success.

Identifying My Internal Barriers To Dreaming Big

Are there other barriers to reaching your goals that are not listed above?

How do you sabotage yourself in pursuit of your dreams?

Do you make excuses for why you cannot pursue your goals? If so, what are the excuses and why do you think you make them?

Circle the excuses below that you find saying to yourself.

- What will people think or say?
- It feels too selfish for me to pursue my dreams.
- My friends will laugh at me.
- I do not deserve my dreams or to be successful. I'm not worthy.

- How can I believe in myself if no one ever believed in me?
- I'm not talented (can't draw, dance, paint, write).
- My ideas are dumb (I am embarrassed, apologetic, or disparaging of the value of my dreams).
- I will upset my partner/mother/father/spouse.
- I'm too... (old, young, uneducated, fat, unfit) to do this.
- I have kids and a family. I can't pursue my dreams.
- I need to be more sensible and pragmatic.
- I'm in school/working so I can't pursue my dreams.
- I need more money in order to do this.
- I'm too busy. I don't have time.
- I have never done this before. I have never seen anyone else like me do this before.
- What if I fail? What if I make a mistake?
- I have a fear of the unknown/risk-taking. I am more comfortable in the familiar. The status quo is safer, and change is risky or dangerous.

How might the barriers you circled come from inside yourself?

Where did these internal messages originate?

What are some strategies to counter these negative messages?

Later when you gather together your Goal Objects, you will find your display becomes a safe place to go where you can work on silencing negative internal voices. Whatever you focus on, positive or negative, will grow stronger in your life. Therefore, it makes sense to give attention to internal messages that are positive affirmations. Do not waste time focusing on things that get you nowhere or over which you have no control. Every step you take should increase, not decrease, the extent of your possibilities.

External Barriers

Besides internal barriers, you may experience external obstacles when pursuing your goals. Sometimes it may be a situation that temporarily holds you back (illness, loss of a job, natural disaster). At other times, a person may let the air out of your balloon and diminish your enthusiasm. We all have these people and situations in our lives. However, what you choose to do with them is what you can control.

Internally, you can change negative thoughts to positive ones. Externally, you can identify barriers and then strategize how to avoid them or deal with them. Identifying and addressing barriers will give you power and free you up to work on reaching your full potential. You can control being around negative people and change your environment.

Write down the external barriers, roadblocks, difficulties, and dream crushers that diminish your spirit and sidetrack the journey to your dreams.

Identifying My External Barriers To Dreaming Big

What are the external barriers to your dreams?

Now that you have identified internal and external barriers, let's strategize about how to use your superpowers to tackle them!

Tackling My Barriers

1. In one or two sentences, write down a barrier (internal or external) or situation that most bugs you, consumes your time or feels like a personal hindrance in pursuing your goals.

2. Write a specific, successful outcome for this barrier or situation. Be creative. In other words, what would need to happen for you to check this problem off your barrier list or stop worrying about it at night?

3. Write down the next action required to move this outcome forward. If you had nothing else to do in your life right now except work on resolution or closure, what concrete action(s) would you take?

How do you feel right now? Is a weight or burden beginning to lift? What did you learn about yourself after answering these questions? What's stopping you right now from taking action? Are the consequences greater for you if an action is taken or if no action is taken? No action also creates consequences—most often it keeps you in the holding pattern you are in.

Tackling My Fear

1. What is something you would like to do but have never done before?

2. What is the specific fear you feel about pursuing this goal? Why?

Handling Setbacks

If you do not reach your goal on the first attempt, how do you react? What is your normal fallback response when you are not successful in the way you think you should be?

What can you learn about yourself from the way you respond to setbacks?

Does your reaction help you, or create more obstacles?

What would you like to change about the way you respond to setbacks? What would that look like?

Because you are becoming more mindful in your life, you now know you are at an amazing juncture on the road to achieving your goals. The trick is to stay positive as you move away from your setbacks and roadblocks. If you find yourself saying, "This is scary," substitute the word *scary* with *exciting*. If you say, "I'm afraid because I don't know what it will feel like," substitute the words, "It may be exhilarating and fulfilling to be in a new place. There is so much potential out there." Listen to your words because they impact your thoughts, and your thoughts impact your actions. Your actions, in turn, propel you towards your goals.

You have now completed the hard work in STEP 1. You should have a clearer understanding of your short- and long-term goals, the supportive people and resources around you, the skills needed to tackle your barriers, and a timeline for reaching your goals.

You will take all that knowledge onto STEP 2: FINDING GOAL OBJECTS to represent your goals and a container for your GO! display.

STEP 2

Finding Your Goal Objects and Container

In STEP 1, you began writing down your hopes and dreams. You explored the internal and external barriers to reaching your dreams. Keep this information close by. You will want to revisit it from time to time as you add to, refine, and reprioritize your thoughts. You will also want to refer to it as you begin this next step of creating your collection of Goal Objects.

Step 2: Objectives

1. **Gather Goal Objects** to put into your display. Think about the symbolism of different objects. If hiking in nature energizes you, a pinecone or bit of moss might represent the outdoors in your display. If you love to dance, a ticket stub from a concert, a miniature dancing shoe from a doll, or a small statue of a dancer might work. Christmas ornaments are a great source of objects because they are small and come in a wide variety of themes.

(continued...)

> ## Step 2: Objectives
> *(continued)*
>
> Find objects to represent:
> - Your dreams and goals (the actual thing you want);
> - The resources to make it happen (people, support, skills, time, money).
>
> 2. **Find a container.** Think about the symbolism of the different kinds of vessels to use. Look for containers at thrift stores or craft outlets, or find them from around your own home, or from family and friends.

The Power of Objects Together

Your display of objects representing your goals is powerful. Part of the power comes from "selective attention." By regularly focusing on the objects and what they mean to you, your attention shifts from extraneous stimuli towards your goals. Additionally, as you contemplate your goals through these representative items, they begin to seem more tangible and real. You find you want to create the circumstances to make your goals happen. Although you may not know everything right now about how to achieve your goals, those kinds of details fall into place as you go through the activities and focus daily on your Goal Objects.

> *The future belongs to those who believe in the beauty of their dreams.*
> ELEANOR ROOSEVELT

Objects and Symbolism

In this step, you will be piecing together seemingly unrelated yet symbolic objects until a kind of narrative emerges. Staying open and mindful during this process will help you see the big picture and how each object relates to the others to tell a story. Your story. Think of them as *ambition action figures!*

Let's talk about the specific types of objects you might want to include in your display.

When looking for objects, don't worry if you find something that seemed perfect at first, but then changed its appeal to you over time. Your needs and interests will morph as you go along. Ideas and objects will come and go until you find the right fit. Your dreams—and hence the objects representing them—will become clearer with time.

For some, the Goal Objects may include religious icons and symbols (e.g., a crucifix, the Star of David, Buddha, Our Lady of Guadalupe). Others find their spiritual connection in nature and include objects such as leaves, a rock, or a small tree branch. The display looks and feels different for each person.

Your objects can symbolize different things: life events, animals, locations, activities, sports, hobbies, family, or friends. They can represent a person, place, or thing. They can be figurines, photos, or souvenirs. They can be purchased from a store or homemade. Collectively, they can convey an abstract concept such as a feeling (joy, happiness). They can also tell a story or paint a picture of a world where this dream comes true and the goal is achieved.

Select things that bring a smile to your face. There is no limit to what can be in your Goal Objects' display. It can contain objects as diverse as a coin, feather, stick, shell, or even a ticket stub. Your GO! display doesn't have to be serious. It can be playful, eclectic, or eccentric, such as sheet music made into a mobile that hangs above your bed (representing your desire to be a professional musician) or a snowboarder figure glued to the top of a wildly colored helmet (you are going to compete in the Winter Olympics someday).

Feel free to include multidimensional objects that incorporate all five senses: smells (apples, incense, essential oils); hearing (water fountain, music, bells, wind chimes); sight (pleasing container, colors that elicit emotions, photos); taste (having tea as you sit by your Goal Objects); and touch (leaves, shells, textures, soft items).

Many cultures, both past and present, attach symbolic meanings to certain objects. Understanding this cultural interpretation may be helpful as you determine which Goal Objects to use. In the Appendix, you will find a list that highlights various cultural beliefs about objects, colors, and symbols and what they represent. You may find this is a useful reference as you gather your objects. However, do not feel bound by these definitions. You may have a completely different feeling or cultural interpretation than is presented and that's fine. This is your collection. Objects, shapes, and colors mean different things to different people.

The Symbolism of My Objects

Describe each Goal Object you plan to put in your GO! display and how that brings you joy or is meaningful to you.

What goal does the object represent?

How will the object give you inspiration and energy to pursue your goal?

At this point in STEP 2, I hope you are jazzed and ready to get up from your comfy chair and take a field trip to start finding your Goal Objects. This hunting and gathering process in itself can be an enlightening adventure. Identify where you will need to go to get the objects you want. It might be a walk in the woods or on the beach. It could be checking out a local thrift shop or craft store. You might explore your home for meaningful trinkets. You might search a holiday store for small, themed ornaments. Maybe it's time for a visit to a special place or to ask a relative to open an old family trunk.

The Meaning of the Goal Objects' Container

You can use any kind of container that feels right to you. It can be any size or shape. However, how you arrange or display the objects may dictate the type of container you choose. Some women and girls may not even use a container, instead choosing to display their Goal Objects on a table or in an open space they see every day. It's up to you.

I generally suggest a small, portable GO! container. A grouping of Goal Objects that can fit into something small can fit in a purse or backpack and can be displayed in any setting. A small collection also works well when space is limited. The display can fit under a bed or in a dresser drawer. A small container (like a shoebox) works well for a young woman going off to school, camp, or a special retreat. It also fits a mobile lifestyle, living in a tiny house, or for mothers who can only find small snippets of quiet time in a corner of a room. A small box can represent big dreams.

Here are some ideas for your container:
- shoebox
- bowl
- basket
- bark
- flat stone
- wooden box
- tiny cabinet

yogurt container

plate

muffin tin

bag or small suitcase

metal mint tin

tray

cloth

Some women and girls take a photo of their Goal Objects and use it as their screen saver or homepage on their cell phone or computer. That way, they see it everywhere they go. Some may put their object on a keyring.

Just like the objects themselves, the physical structure or vessel you select can also be symbolic and convey a message or feeling. You can decide what you want your container to symbolize, or maybe the container is simply the right size for your objects and space. Either way is fine. The important thing is the symbolism of the objects.

Here are some ideas about container symbolism.

> **Bowls and baskets** often represent warmth, nurturing, encompassing, nourishing, sustenance, and the act of gathering.
>
> **Boxes** represent things that are orderly, self-contained, or unknown and mysterious; boxes that open symbolize awakening.
>
> **Cloth** can represent wrapping yourself in love, warmth, and comfort.
>
> **Jars** symbolize carrying food or water to feed and nourish.
>
> **A vase** can symbolize the soul or womb.

A flat object, like a plate, tray, or rock, can represent your openness to the world and to opportunities. Plates also represent sustenance and nourishment.

A few years ago, I created my own GO! display that I hang on the wall by my office desk. I see it every morning. It inspires me, makes me smile, and keeps me on track. I bought a small twelve-by-twelve-inch white wooden cabinet at a thrift store for $3.99. My find has a glass door and five compartments. On the top of the cabinet, four index cards, propped up by wire picture holders, state my goals along with pictures of the goals attached to the card. Below the cabinet are objects representing the support, resources, and skills in my life that will help me reach my goals.

The center compartment of the display box represents me: my interests, personality, and skills. A small key with the label "compassion" dangles on the knob that opens the compartment door. I do not want to do anything in life without compassion. The inside of the compartment is painted a happy, Kermit-the-Frog green because I want to be joyful and live a green, earth-friendly life. Suspended from the top of the compartment is an ornament given to me by a good friend years ago that depicts a smiling woman soaring through the air, wearing pearls, and holding a newspaper, phone, and briefcase. Her golden hair sparkles with glitter and she wears commanding black boots. I like the juxtaposition of the parts of her strong persona. She presents a joyful image of a successful, empowered, and free-spirited woman. She works hard and has a zest for life. She seems to have it all with great ease and control. She is alive and exuding joie de vivre. She doesn't appear too stressed either.

I want to be that soaring woman. On the walls of the center compartment hang a miniature suitcase, passport, laptop computer, and some tiny airplane tickets I found at a craft store. On the bottom is white sand that I brought back from a trip. The flying non-stressed woman is at the beach—a place where I feel reflective and relaxed. I believe some people are mountain people and some are beach people, just like there are cat or dog people. I personally like the beach. In the sand are words made from wire that I find motivating: hope, create, believe, dream, inspire.

Surrounding the center compartment are four separate compartments. Each represents positive aspects in my life—the people and resources that can help me reach my dreams. They are the things that boost me, provide encouragement, and give emotional and physical support. One compartment is painted yellow for sunlight and represents my friends. Inside that compartment is a purple heart-shaped rock that I painted with my closest friends' names. These friends are always there for me. They are my rock. Some I have known most of my life, others only a year or two, but all are honest, positive, and nontoxic. Being with them gives me comfort and doesn't require an effort. We have laughed together over silly things and shared the processing of private pain like the loss of a parent, a marriage, or estrogen. A small toy telephone dangles from the top of that compartment because I know I can call any of them, any time of day, if I need them.

The compartment below that one represents my spiritual support. It is painted fuchsia for gentility and contains a miniature statue of Ganesh, the Hindu deity widely revered as the remover of obstacles in one's life. His elephant-like head symbolizes new beginnings, the arts and sciences, intellect, and wisdom. Ganesh is also considered the patron of writing. Since I scribe for much of my living and some of my goals involve writing, I appreciate his watchful eye over my keyboard.

The third compartment is painted navy blue and contains objects from my father. He died in 1991 and was my biggest cheerleader. A smart, self-made man, he was not afraid to try new things. In hindsight, he was truly a feminist. My father encouraged my sister and me to be assertive, to get an education, and to do whatever we wanted to do (she became a minister and I went into criminal justice). His navy-blue truck was always full of tools and projects. Next to his plaid Herculon recliner in our family room, he kept sketches and drawings of creative endeavors he wanted to tackle. Not only was he a dreamer, but he made his dreams come true. Family and friends have told me through the years how I remind them of my father. I beam when I hear that, since I am honored to have known him and share his DNA. I carry his spirit with me, in my display, and in the pursuit of my passions.

The last compartment, painted red for love and passion, contains pictures of my husband, Andy. The role we play in each other's lives is truly a gift and frosting on the cake. Our relationship brings me pure joy. I see his support through his respect and actions. I feel lightness through his words and humor. He supports me every day in the pursuit of my goals and dreams.

The container you choose can be part of the symbolism in your Goal Objects' display. Spend some time thinking about what size and shape will work for you.

Before you move on to STEP 3, find your Goal Objects and select a display container.

> *"Go confidently in the direction of your dreams.
> Live the life you've imagined."*
> HENRY DAVID THOREAU

STEP 3

Creating and Staging Your Goal Objects

> ### Step 3: Objectives
> 1. Decorate your container.
> 2. Place the Goal Objects in the container.
> 3. Find an appropriate location for the container.

Emma was a fourteen-year-old girl in one of my workshops. She wanted to be a veterinarian. The GO! visualization exercises allowed her, for the first time, to think about what it would actually take to get to her goal. As she collected her Goal Objects (small animal figurines to represent her dream) and did the activities, she became mindful and strategic about the necessary steps ahead. Her goal to be a veterinarian became real and concrete. She started thinking about her Action Plan: how she could get help with math; when she could talk to her aunt who had offered to help pay for her college; how she could get some practical experience working with animals. She put her Goal Objects into a special container—a plastic dog dish with two bowls.

What an appropriate container for a veterinarian-to-be! One side of the dish had dog food in it, representing her love and caring for animals. The other side was filled with pennies, representing the supportive people and resources she needed around her. Little ceramic animals and cards with action steps written on them were placed throughout the GO! display. She moved from wishing to be a veterinarian (a passive action) to concrete, strategic goal setting (an active endeavor).

I love Emma's story. She put serious cognitive energy into selecting just the right symbolic objects for her situation and finding a fitting container. The process also clarified for her the next steps on her quest.

Goal Objects: Simplifying and Prioritizing

In PART I, we covered challenges around time management and prioritizing as a barrier for some women. Now that you have started putting your Goal Objects together, other issues may have surfaced. As you begin to regularly think about your goals and the specific steps to reach them, figuring out what to do with these issues will become easier. This concentration and focus shuts out many issues such as unnecessary emotional and physical clutter in your life. It forces you to hone in on what you need in order to create the future you want.

Have you ever had to evacuate your home to escape a fire? The skill of laser-like prioritizing plays a key part. Most people describe that experience as life changing and illuminating. In the midst of a fire, they looked around their home, and after making sure all the humans and pets were safe, experienced sharp decision-making that surprised them. Their brain became hyper-focused and made important, split-second decisions about what to protect and take with them. They saved such things as photo albums, a cherished gift from their spouse, a souvenir from a trip, a scarf from a beloved relative. The rest, when it got down to it, was meaningless. I experienced those same intense reactions when a housefire happened to me. Observing a primal survival skill kick in was both amazing and frightening. This is the kind of clear mindset you hope to experience when focusing on your Goal Objects.

People who prioritize like this are able to skip over the mundane, the replaceable, the things without emotional connection. They literally wrap their arms around objects associated with a positive memory or special meaning—not something special to the Smiths next door, or to their teacher, or to the firefighters. They ignore things that symbolize sadness, disappointment, or fear. They grab things that are joyful and meaningful to them. As you create your own GO! display, ask yourself, with that same firefighters-at-my-door precision, "What is important to me? What is meaningful to me? What brings me joy?"

Turn back to the two exercises in STEP 1, *What do you want for yourself?* and *What are your short-term and long-term goals?* Look at what you wrote in those activities. Then take a few minutes to think about the fire scenario above. Is there anything on the lists you would now add, change, or prioritize differently?

Decorate Your Container

After finding a container for your Goal Objects, you may want to embellish it in some way. For instance, one woman in a workshop had a wooden box with four quadrants representing the strength of the four winds in Native American culture. Another woman had a shoebox with three distinct areas, a right-brain area for her intuitive/holistic strengths, a left-brain area for her logical/analytical/rational strengths, and a middle area for her goals. Another woman glued clippings of favorite quotes and fortune cookie messages to the bottom of a bowl. She put Goal Objects into the bowl. The good fortune resonated up through the objects depicting her goals. Another participant placed objects symbolizing roots and wings into a small painted wooden birdhouse, reminding her to stay grounded but allowing her to fly. A different woman placed objects representing her goals in the middle of a lidded plastic storage box, surrounded by photos of people in her life who could help her reach those goals. One of my favorite containers transformed a simple muffin tin into a dozen miniature scenes depicting the steps in one woman's twelve-month Action Plan to set up a food truck. The last muffin slot displayed her goal.

Find a table or creative space to work on your container. Assemble magazines, glue, colored paper, scissors, paints, and other materials you may need to decorate your vessel. Since it takes time for paint or glue to dry, feel free to work on your display a little bit at a time.

Begin painting, shaping, and embellishing your container as much or as little as you like. If particular words inspire you, paint or adhere the words to your container or on the objects themselves. I often see words and phrases such as believe, love, passion, dream big, energy, go for it, get 'er done.

Continue creating, decorating, and filling your container. Remember, there is no right way to create or decorate this new home for your treasured objects. Like you, it is unique.

The creative decorating time also offers a rich opportunity for contemplation. You may decide to do this activity alone or with others. Think about the following questions as you work on your container:

1. What do you think of the phrase: You've got to dream it before it can happen?

2. What things feed you, inspire you, make you smile, create an experience of joy or bliss?

3. Why do you believe you can accomplish your dreams? (Remember to focus on positive things, not negative ones.)

4. How can you chunk your dream to make it more manageable and less overwhelming? That is, tackle it in a series of small steps, with multiple successes and immediate rewards. Create milestones to propel momentum, monitor progress, and make mid-course adjustments.

Don't forget the mindful part of this activity. As you work on your container, think about how you feel in the moment. Are there particular discussion questions that resonate with you or Goal Objects or activities that bring you the most fulfillment? Is there a feeling of anticipation or excitement over the possibilities that lie ahead? Gravitate towards this energy as you create the container that will house and protect your goals.

You may want to name your Goal Objects' display or container if a theme emerges. For instance, your theme might be "The Year of Getting Out of Debt", "Getting Healthy", "Starting My Business", "Finishing School", or "Adopting a Child."

Putting Final Objects into Your Display

As you place the final objects into your GO! display, honor the special, sacred space you've created for yourself. Look at all the Goal Objects. What do they say *to* you? What do they say *about* you? What are some of the feelings associated with your new collection? Think about each object and all the positive energy and creative work that went into making it.

Note that this final step can be an emotional experience. You are one step closer to your dreams! You are giving your dreams intention and attention. These exercises may have brought up memories of negative experiences that are now replaced with positive ones. Experiencing a cocktail of emotions is normal and speaks to the power of the Goal Objects' experience. Embrace your feelings—don't ignore them—and know they are cleansing, cathartic, and part of harnessing your own power.

Where to Locate Your Display of Objects

Your new GO! display will be a place to go that offers grounding and inspiration. It is a place to meditate and visualize your goals and dreams. You may find it takes on a feeling of sacred space. Your creation possesses inherent energy.

It is now time to think about where to put your display. Its size and shape may dictate its location. Some typical places include a wall, desk, nightstand, tabletop, car, or dresser. You can keep it in a drawer, closet, or secret location. It can be in your office, studio, kitchen, or by the door so you see it coming and going. It should be in a place where it can be viewed easily every day.

Additionally, always have your Goal Objects in front of you. This represents the future. Look around where you live or work and find a place that you can face to locate your display.

Another option is to take a photo of your Goal Objects or create a mini version of it to carry with you in your day planner, suitcase, briefcase, purse, or backpack. The photo can serve as a screen saver on your computer or cell phone.

Many people believe the placement of things affects the dynamics of energy flow. You may want to consider the location of your display as it relates to positive spirit and vitality. For example, the ancient Chinese practice of feng shui, Celtic principles, and Native American beliefs suggest that the location of something correlates with its intent and energy. Here are some suggestions for locations and what they mean.

DIRECTION	Native American	Chinese Feng Shui	Celtic Principles	Other Beliefs
NORTH	wisdom, thought	adaptable, charm, creativity, social ability, wit	earth, home, security, fertility	abundance, wealth & prosperity (energy, spirituality—northeast)
SOUTH	beginnings, purity	physical strength, health, adventure, loyalty	fire, energy, passion, creativity	work, career, fame, recognition (support of people, universal support—southwest)
EAST	salvation, spirit	trust, sincerity, love, compassion	air, communication, new beginnings, new growth	health, safety, well-being (life changes, transformation—southeast)
WEST	conclusions, fullness	confidence, busness, energy, persistence	water, emotion, psyche, movement	creativity, intelligence knowledge (relationships, connection, marriage—northwest)

Some spiritual practices associate directions with time:

    North – *infinity*

    South – *the present*

    East – *the future*

    West – *the past*

Wherever you locate your Goal Objects, you may need to establish ground rules or courtesies with others in your household or workplace. For instance, you may not want others to touch your Goal Objects or even see them. You may not want them dusted or moved in any way. You may want your display to be visible to others so they can see what you are doing and support you. The decision is yours. Remember, you are the caretaker of this precious exhibit. Make sure others know the importance of your Goal Objects and your expectations.

Location of My GO! Objects

Where do you want to put your Goal Objects' display or container?

Before you move on to STEP 4, the final step, your container needs to be decorated and the Goal Objects put inside. You should also have a location picked out where the GO! display will reside.

STEP 4

Your Action Plan

Goals are dreams with deadlines.
NAPOLEON HILL, "THINK AND GROW RICH"

In STEP 3, we reviewed where to locate your GO! display. I hope by now you have found a peaceful spot that creates a comfortable place to reflect, meditate, and evaluate your goals and dreams.

> ### Step 4: Objectives
> 1. Develop your goal Action Plan.
> 2. Create a ritual/routine to do at your display to help you visualize and focus on your goals and dreams.

In this final step, we discuss what to do at the display in order to help you visualize your goals and dreams. We will also address how to get those great ideas out of your head and into fruition via an Action Plan. Dreams don't work unless you do.

The first task is to formalize your Action Plan. Get everything written down into a step-by-step strategy with a timeline. People who write down their goals and develop an Action Plan are more likely to achieve them than those who do not.

Some people develop, fine-tune, or work on their Action Plan at the same time they are visualizing their goals at their display. Others contemplate an Action Plan they completed prior to the goal visualization process. In either case, use this time to think strategically, identifying the path you want to take, giving yourself permission to deviate if you discover a new or better way to proceed. Mindfulness is about being awake to all possibilities.

The Action Plan is your instructional manual to go along with the objects. Below is a sample Action Plan form completed by a woman who wants to open her own food truck. You can see the amount of detail she has developed in order to make her plan come to fruition. Below her plan is a blank form for you to use for your own goals. Feel free to use this form or create your own Action Plan process. Refer to the activities you completed in Steps 1 to 3 for ideas and information.

Start your Action Plan by writing down detailed steps outlining how you are going to accomplish your goal(s). In the far-left column, write down the tasks you need to complete to reach your goals. List the tasks in sequence. The more detailed the plan, the greater the chance that nothing will be overlooked. Additional tasks will inevitably emerge as you start devising your plan, so leave space or create the plan on the computer so adjustments and insertions can be made easily.

The next column to the right is a place to list the resources you'll need to complete the task. For instance, doing research on licenses for the food truck or making calls may just take time. Rather than simply writing in "time" as a needed resource, estimate how much time will be needed (e.g., six hours). Likewise, estimate the cost of an item, such as "$5,000 for graphic design services/logo and business cards," rather than just saying "money" (round up because things are often more expensive than expected).

The next column is the timeline. When do you plan to work on the task? When will the task be completed? Some tasks may take a day; others may take months.

In the far-right column, indicate the Goal Object that corresponds to that step or goal. Some women and girls have a single object represent the overall goal while others use an object for each step. In the example here, the object (a tiny toy food truck) is used for several steps. A Susan B. Anthony silver dollar is used as the Goal Object whenever the step requires monetary resources.

On the following page is a sample Action Plan that may help you complete your own form.

Sample Action Plan

GOAL: Operate my own food truck selling cupcakes

Steps / Tasks	Resources	Timeline	Goal Object
Contact state commerce/corporation department to determine laws and regulations that apply to food trucks. This includes identifying all licenses and permits needed.	6 hours of time to make calls and do background research.	Month 1	Toy food truck
Drive to area where other food trucks congregate. Talk to other food truck operators to ascertain useful tips about this kind of business. Go to website or call to get information.	10 hours of time. Car/gas.	Month 1	Toy food truck Silver dollar
Methodically go through each regulation to determine cost and feasibility. Create a checklist.	7 hours of time for background research.	Month 1	Toy food truck Silver dollar
Select name for business. Conduct a focus group for business name and concept. Find graphic designer for logo.	Prep, on-site setup for focus group. 6 hours of time and $500 for business cards, logo, graphic design services	Months 1 - 2	Toy food truck Silver dollar
Look into overhead and startup costs: truck, painting logo on truck, food ingredients, needed vendors, business license, insurance, marketing including website and social media, materials, labor, health inspections, legal/LLC paperwork, land to park truck, contracts.	12 hours of time to make calls and do background research for setup logistics. Money needed for truck purchase, startup legal costs, kitchen equipment and supplies, food ingredients and insurance. Estimated $50,000.	Months 1 - 2	Toy food truck Silver dollar
Develop a business plan and cost-benefit analysis. Work with local community college and/or Small Business Administration for help in development and review of plan.	30 hours of time.	Month 3	Toy food truck Silver dollar
Buy truck. Hire graphic artist to do logo design on side of truck. Take truck to paint shop.	$8,000 to paint truck	Months 4 - 5	Toy food truck Silver dollar
Practice recipes, logistics, and setup. Conduct a soft opening.	40 hours of time. Money TBD if employees need to be hired.	Month 6	Toy food truck Silver dollar

My Action Plan

GOAL:

Steps / Tasks	Resources	Timeline	Goal Object

What to Do at Your GO! Display

You can create your own Goal Objects' experience that is right for you. Some women and girls design a daily or weekly routine that directs their attention on their goals (e.g., every Monday morning). Whatever you decide, the routine needs to fit your world and your personality in order to work.

Many women and girls use the following routine when they are at their GO! display:

1. Establish a ritual;

2. Set your intention and concentrate on the meaning/symbolism of the Goal Objects;

3. Relax/de-stress;

4. Visualize success and your dreams coming true. Think about your Action Plan and put energy into the specific steps to make your goals come to fruition.

Besides visualizing the outcome (the goal itself), you can also visualize the process (each step) to get you there. Imagine successfully completing each step before moving to the next. Picture a successful outcome at each step. Many women report this visualization process takes the apprehension out of making that cold call or walking into a room to network.

Let's discuss each part of this routine.

1. Establish a Ritual

Select a routine, ritual, ceremony, or practice that provides for a start and finish to your contemplative time. This could be anything special such as lighting a candle, dimming lights, arranging fresh flowers, playing music, putting on headphones, burning incense, singing, sitting a certain way facing the objects, closing the door for alone time, or ringing a bell. It can also be as simple as pausing for a moment at your display. For me, every morning when I arrive at my desk, I light a candle, say an affirming phrase about trying to connect my head with my heart in my work and in my life, look at my Goal Objects in their wooden box on the wall, and think about everything the GO! display means to me. The few minutes this takes reinforces how I want the day to unfold.

Rituals create a safe resting place for a busy and complicated life. A display of Goal Objects represents a place where you can dump those things that weigh you down, allowing you to reenergize. Some women and girls opt to write in a journal and incorporate that into their ritual. You may want to keep a special notebook nearby to jot down thoughts and ideas, your Action Plan, or keep a volume of inspirational readings handy.

My Routine at My GO! Display

What rituals or routines will you incorporate at your display of Goal Objects?

If you bring the right earnestness and grace to your ceremony, you will derive many benefits from the experience.

2. Set Your Intention

Every time you pause at your GO! display, start with setting your intention. Be clear about what you want out of the experience with the objects and subsequently, with your goals. Think or say affirmations related to your goals using phrases in present tense, such as, "I am capable of learning French," instead of "I hope to be able to learn French at some point." Say, "I am opening up my food truck this June" instead of "I hope I can figure out how to open a food truck." This approach solidifies your intention and commitment and allows you to move forward with confidence.

In addition to setting your intention in a quiet personal way at your display, you may want to let others know about your dreams and your plans to reach your goals. You have now surrounded yourself with supportive people who you trust and will be there for you. Master the thirty-second sound-bite pitch so you can easily describe to others what you are doing. Tell them about your plans and even your Goal Objects if you wish. This is a good way to get support and accountability.

You can also set intention with others by having a ceremony related to your specific goals. Creative and meaningful intention rituals are endless. If your dream is to open an animal rescue shelter, arrange to have a picnic for family and friends at the zoo announcing your intention. Have a ribbon cutting ceremony at your new home gym to set your intention to exercise more for a healthier lifestyle. Throw a party with bluegrass music to announce your intention to learn to play the mandolin and move to Nashville. Cut up credit cards, burn slips of paper with obstacles written on them, hold a funeral and burial for your cigarettes, or smash a candy dish with a hammer. Who knew setting your intention could be this much fun?

This kind of public intention ritual might even generate some great Goal Objects to bring back to your display, such as your ticket stub from the zoo, a piece of the destroyed credit card, a cigarette butt, or the ribbon from your new gym opening.

> **Setting My Intention**
>
> How might you set your intention to reach your goals?
>
> At your display:
>
> Publicly:

3. Relax and De-Stress

Enjoy the solitude with your Goal Objects. This is the moment to cherish and rejuvenate. Give yourself permission to take this time slowly. Women and girls often don't allow themselves downtime to just be and think about their future. We tend to carry all our personal issues and responsibilities wherever we go. The journey to your goals has very little space in the overhead bin for all your, and everyone else's, baggage. Small carry-on luggage of personal issues is fine. We all have those. But now you have examined your life, identified and embraced your goals, and are ready to zip up that big old suitcase of negative issues and put it away.

When you pause in front of your Goal Objects, you are investing in your future while honoring the past and present. It is a place to draw sustenance, peace, and inspiration. You have created a transcendent place for positive thought and energy.

De-stressing and relaxing where your Goal Objects reside is important for concentration. Begin by focusing on your breath. Take slow, deep breaths, inhaling through your nose and slowly exhaling through your mouth. Pause at the top of the breath and the bottom of the breath. Relax your shoulders away from your ears, think about each part of your body with each breath and release stress from that area. When you feel calm and undistracted by life and the things around you, begin to focus on your goals and dreams. How do you feel now? Do your dreams bring you joy? Do they feel within reach? Feel where the emotions have rested in your body—from the lump in your throat, the smile on your face, the release of worry in your brow, the goosebumps on your arm, or the tingling and wiggling of your big toe. Dreams possess more power when they are embedded in the head, heart, and whole body.

Relax and De-stress

How will you relax and de-stress at your Goal Objects' ("GO!") display?

4. Visualize and Plan

Visualize success! What would be reaching your goals look and feel like? Create a detailed image in your mind of your goal(s) using all five senses (hearing, taste, touch, sight, smell). If your goal is to be an ice skater at the Olympics, visualize completing your best skating routine ever, looking at the international judges holding up their score cards giving you high marks. You worked hard to get there. You earned it. You should feel proud of yourself. Hold that image in your mind as long as you can. How do you feel seeing your winning scores? Hearing the roar of the crowd? Feeling the hugs from your teammates and family? Imagine the thrill of standing on the awards' podium, bending over and smelling the bouquet of red roses and seeing the shiny metal being placed around your neck? Maybe even tasting a glass of sparkly champagne?

Some people pick a single Goal Object or one step from the Action Plan to reflect on and visualize while at their display. Try to create a mental image of this future event. Can you see yourself in a place and time where that dream becomes a reality? Imagine yourself in that new role or location. What is that like for you?

The more time you spend with your Goal Objects, the more your goals will feel tangible and within reach. Before you can believe and achieve your goals, you first must envision what they look like. Visualization doesn't guarantee success, nor does it substitute for hard work and determination. But when combined with mindfulness, self-reflection, awareness of roadblocks, and diligence to your path, you have the power to recapture your goals and dreams.

Many women and girls get stuck at the implementation stage. We all have good intentions, but without a plan, follow-through won't happen. As you are visualizing success, take the specific steps from your Action Plan and commit to completing one step today, tomorrow and the next day. You are on your way.

No dream is too small, no dream is too big. Follow your heart and your dreams can change the world.
AUTHOR UNKNOWN

You've done it!

You've completed the four important steps to reach your goals. You have set the foundation for success. You have visualized your dreams and they are right in front of you. Now, as you look at your Goal Objects every day, you are mindful. You can see yourself winning, flying, surfing, mothering, graduating, and being the best you can be. You can do this. No more dream drain. You can create that amazing life you want.

RATE YOUR PROGRESS TOWARDS YOUR GOALS!

How close are you to reaching your goals? What is holding you back? Take a personal inventory of your strengths and weaknesses, confidence and fears, internal and external roadblocks, and important action steps. Women and girls who are successful at reaching their goals are information-gatherers. Here you go! Rate yourself on your progress and what you still need to do to reach your goals. You may be closer than you think!

Go to **www.marciakmorgan.com** and get a free copy of the worksheet *"How Close am I to Reaching my Goals?"*

Plus be inspired! Download free pictures of other GO! displays while on the site.

WRITE A REVIEW

Thank you for reading **GO! How to Get Going and Achieve Your Goals and Dreams.** I poured my heart and soul into writing this book and compiling rich stories from other women and girls. I can't wait to hear how it helped you reach your goals. If you enjoyed the book, please leave a review online and tell your friends about it. Reviews help the book become more visible. Your review may inspire another woman or girl to get this book and reach her goals.

WORKSHOPS — GROUP

Are you interested in holding a workshop? We can bring the workshop to your city, community or organization!

During these workshops (half day or one day option), participants are guided through the four steps on how to connect with their inner self, the voice that keeps their dreams hidden or set aside. They will explore if they are living the life they want and if not, what they need to do to make a change. They will discover the power of goal objects (GO!) and that they are not alone—other women and girls are asking the same questions. Participants find support from others, potentially form lifetime friendships, and get the encouragement to seize the dreams they deserve.

Workshops can be uniquely designed for your specific needs and interests. Below is a sampling of some of the topics.
- How dreams disappear
- The power of goal objects
- The magic of mindfulness in pursuing your goals
- Exploring your creativity
- Capturing your goals and dreams
- Common roadblocks women and girls face when pursuing their dreams
- Visualization with goal objects
- The 4 Step to Reaching your Goals

>Step 1: Identifying your Goals and Dreams
>
>Step 2: Finding your Goal Objects and Container
>
>Step 3: Creating and Staging your Goal Objects
>
>Step 4: Your Action Plan

Additional workshops on gender issues (socialization, female psychosocial development, gender and crime, etc.) are also available.

The workshop audience can be as small as five or as large as 500. Marcia is also available to meet with the media upon request. For questions or a quote, please contact Marcia at **www.marciakmorgan.com/workshops**.

WORKSHOPS — INDIVIDUAL

Who knew going after your goals could be so fun and rewarding? Individual workshops are available online offering personal, one-on-one attention. The topics covered are basically the same as if you attended a larger group workshop but can be customized to better meet your specific needs.

Typically, these workshops are conducted over visual telephone calls (such as "Skype" of "Facetime"). You'll be given a reading assignment to be completed before the first session. Each session is guided with interactive discussion. Individual workshops can be a cost-effective way to learn and have fun because they do not take a large amount of time away from other obligations. Additionally, there are no expenses such as transportation, lodging and food costs associated with travel to a traditional workshop site.

Don't put off your dreams any longer!
Contact Marcia to set up an individual or online workshop at
www.marciakmorgan.com/workshops

SPEAKING ENGAGEMENTS

Please contact me at **marcia@migima.com** if you're interested in having me speak to your group, conference, or organization.

Additional copies of **GO! How to Get Going and Achieve Your Goals and Dreams**, and other books by this author, are available online and through bookstores.

Appendix

APPENDIX

Symbolism of Colors, Shapes, and Objects

Below is a sampling of characteristics, emotions, and feelings you may want to incorporate into your GO! display. One way to do that is to use colors, numbers, animals, plants, or food that symbolize the characteristic you want to convey. This list is a compilation of things from various cultural beliefs and practices. Since this is only a partial list to get you started, you are encouraged to go online to find additional things to represent the characteristics you want to include in your display.

COURAGE AND STRENGTH

Color: orange, red
Numbers: one, ten
Nature (plants and trees): cedar, oak, columbine, mahogany
Nature (stones, gems, shells, metal): diamond, garnet, ruby, titanium, iron, labradorite, morganite
Animals: bull, badger, tiger, lion, bear, griffin, boar
Food, Spices, Herbs, Oils: sandalwood, thyme, garlic, black cohosh, tobacco

STABILITY

Color: brown, green, black, all earth colors
Shapes: triangle, three legs, djed, pillar
Numbers: four, eight
Nature (plants and trees): oak, ivy, moss, petrified wood
Nature (stones, gems. shells, metal): coal, copper, emerald, peridot, salt, green tourmaline
Animals: wolf, bear, stag, bison, horse
Food, Spices, Herbs, Oils: sage, corn, potatoes, salt from ocean

COMFORT, RELAXATION, HARMONY AND PEACE
Color: brown, blue, green, pink
Shapes: triangle, peace symbol, "z"
Numbers: two, four
Nature (plants and trees): birch, petunias, apple blossoms, evergreen, bonsai tree, palm tree
Nature (stones, gems, shells, metals): aquamarine, emerald
Animals: dove, dog, bluebird
Food, Spices, Herbs, Oils: olive, sandalwood, bergamot, chamomile, parsley, tuberose

JOY, HAPPINESS, OPTIMISM, AND KINDNESS
Color: orange, yellow, rainbow
Shapes: star, hearts
Numbers: two, three
Nature (plants and trees): alder, maple, sunflowers, azalea
Nature (stones, gems and shells): agate, sapphire
Animals: otter, unicorn, hedgehog
Food, Spices, Herbs, Oils: lime, orange

HOPE
Color: pink, green, blue
Shapes: anchor, heart, closed box
Numbers: three
Nature (plants and trees): chrysanthemums, iris, bachelor buttons, fruit trees, ginkgo tree
Nature (stones, gems and shells): opal, ocean shells
Animals: dove, butterflies, fish
Food, Spices, Herbs, Oils: mustard seed, pineapple

ACTION AND ENERGY
Color: orange, red
Shapes: spiral, letters E or U
Numbers: one, six, eight
Nature (plants and trees): copaiba tree, sequoia
Nature (stones, gems and shells): lapis
Animals: cheetah, beaver
Food, Spices, Herbs, Oils: apple, ginger, pepper, mint, vanilla bean

ACHIEVEMENT AND GOALS
Color: turquoise
Shapes: square, star
Numbers: one, seven, ten
Nature (plants and trees): clover
Nature (stones, gems and shells): turquoise, gold, silver, hemimorphite (pink)
Animals: horse (endurance), cardinal bird
Food, Spices, Herbs, Oils: cinnamon, strawberry

TRANSFORMATION AND HEALING
Color: purple, green, blue, white
Shapes: heart, bridge
Numbers: five, ten
Nature (plants and trees): birch, aspen, heather
Nature (stones, gems and shells): jade, peridot, tourmaline, amber
Animals: peacock, dragonfly
Food, Spices, Herbs, Oils: apple, garlic, plum

POWER
Color: black, orange, red, purple
Shapes: circle (wreath), square, pyramid
Numbers: one, two, seven, eight
Nature (plants and trees): ebony
Nature (stones, gems and shells): obsidian, bronzite, jasper
Animals: horse, dragonfly, bull, elephant, lion, bear, cheetah
Food, Spices, Herbs, Oils: meat, rye

WEALTH
Color: gold, green, red
Shapes: infinity symbol, square, dollar sign
Numbers: one, eight
Nature (plants and trees): yellow violates, maple, myrtle, oak, eucalyptus
Nature (stones, gems and shells): gold, jade
Animals: cats, Chinese dragon, boar, fish
Food, Spices, Herbs, Oils: jasmine, alfalfa, bergamot, almond, basil

FERTILITY AND IMMORTALITY
Color: red, green, white, gold
Shapes: ankh, infinity symbol
Numbers: eight
Nature (plants and trees): hay, myrtle
Nature (stones, gems and shells): turquoise, horn
Animals: rabbit, peacock, snake, beetle/scarab
Food, Spices, Herbs, Oils: rice, peach, egg, banana, wheat

PURITY AND ENLIGHTENMENT
Color: white, pink
Shapes: circle, line, star
Numbers: one, seven
Nature (plants and trees): lotus flower, white rose
Nature (stones, gems and shells): tourmaline, azeztulite, diamond
Animals: lamb, unicorn
Food, Spices, Herbs, Oils: grapefruit

FEMININE
Color: pink/rose, white
Shapes: circle, gender symbol for women, crescent moon
Numbers: two
Nature (plants and trees): lilies, water
Nature (stones, gems and shells): pearls, silver, abalone shell/mother of pearl
Animals: unicorns, bird
Food, Spices, Herbs, Oils: apple

REFERENCES

Ben-Shahar, Tal. 2012. *Choose the Life You Want: The Mindful Way to Happiness.* New York: THE EXPERIMENT, LLC.

Brown, Brené. *"The Power of Vulnerability."* Filmed June 2010. TED VIDEO, 20:13. https://www.ted.com/talks/brene_brown_on_vulnerability.

Centers for Disease Control and Prevention.
"Adverse Childhood Experiences (ACE) Study." 1995-97. Page last updated June 14, 2016 https://www.cdc.gov/violenceprevention/acestudy/about.html

Mullainatham, Sendhil, and Eldar Shafir. 2013.
Scarcity: Why Having Too Little Means So Much.
New York: TIME BOOKS, HENRY HOLT AND CO.

Oborne, Abi. *"My Husband; Five Reasons I Am Not Lucky to Have Him."*
Writing about the Reality of Being Mum (blog). HUFFINGTON POST, July 27, 2016.
http://www.huffingtonpost.co.uk/abi-oborne/five-reasons-i-am-not-lucky-to-have-my-husband_b_7875666.html.

Reshman Saujani. *"Teach Girls Bravery, Not Perfection."*
Filmed February 2016. TED video, 12:40.
https://www.ted.com/talks/reshma_saujani_teach_girls_bravery_not_perfection.

TD Bank. 2016. *"Visualizing Goals Influence Health and Happiness."*
Posted August 23, 2016
https://newscenter.td.com/us/en/news/2016/td-study-reveals-the-best-ways-to-say-thanks.

Winfrey, Oprah. 2013. *"Winfrey's Commencement Address"*
(Speech, Harvard University Commencement, Cambridge, MA, May 30, 2013).
THE HARVARD GAZETTE. May 31, 2013
https://news.harvard.edu/gazette/story/2013/05/winfreys-commencement-address/.

ACKNOWLEDGMENTS

Thank you to all the individuals and groups who created their own special Goal Object displays, read drafts of the book, and piloted the activities. Their feedback was incredibly valuable to me: The Women's M Salon; Deevy Holcomb, Andrea Abramson, Barbara Abt, Diane Luckett and Shellie Littau, Girls Circle Leaders, Deschutes County Juvenile Community Justice; The Spirit Sisters, Olympia, Washington; the middle school and high school girls at the "Girls Summit," LaPine, Oregon; dear friends Susan Grover Cooper, attorney and women's health advocate and Martha Samco, artist and colorist extraordinaire; my good-eye-for-details sister, Dana Morgan McBrien; and Deborah McWilliams, PhD, psychotherapist, who met with me multiple times over breakfast during our affectionately called "Pancakes and Prose" sessions. We inspired, constructively critiqued, and motivated each other to create. It was great for my writing but not my waistline.

In my life, I have two amazing stepdaughters, Kristi and Allison, and three granddaughters, Bobbie, Miley, and Hazel. I dedicate this book to these five strong, young women. They bring me inspiration and hope as I watch them pursue their dreams every day. What a treat it has been to watch them navigate their journey into and through womanhood!

Lastly, I want to say thank you to Andy Jordan, my husband and confidante. Andy provided me with love, support, and encouragement to follow my dreams and write this book. How great is it to have a cheerleader who roots for you, a sounding board who listens intently, and someone who bears witness to your life with a constant smile? I love and appreciate him every day.

ABOUT THE AUTHOR

MARCIA KAYE MORGAN brings a wealth of experience helping women and girls reach their potential. Drawing on more than forty years as a national consultant, researcher, trainer and author on gender and crime, this sought-after motivational speaker tackles the casualties of women's dreams in this latest work. In 1976, she and a colleague developed the groundbreaking, anatomically-correct dolls now used around the world to interview victims of child sexual abuse. Marcia initially made her mark heading up one of the first all-female rape investigation programs in the United States. Her related books for professionals and children are highly regarded by national and international organizations.

As the Executive Director of Migima, LLC, since 1980, Marcia oversees an innovative firm that provides high-energy consulting services in criminal justice and social issues. She has written several books and training curricula, as well as conducted workshops on helping women and girls reach their goals. Her work has helped change lives.

Marcia, her husband, and yellow lab live in Bend, Oregon.

OTHER BOOKS BY MARCIA KAYE MORGAN

───────────────

My Feelings

How to Interview Sexual Abuse Victims

SafeTOUCH

www.ingramcontent.com/pod-product-compliance
Lightning Source LLC
Chambersburg PA
CBHW052057110526
44591CB00013B/2246